BLESS THIS HOUSE

by
Margaret M. Fogg

BLESS THIS HOUSE

by
Margaret M. Fogg

Copyright © 2006 Margaret M. Fogg
All Rights Reserved

PUBLISHED BY:
BRENTWOOD CHRISTIAN PRESS
4000 BEALLWOOD AVENUE
COLUMBUS, GEORGIA 31904

exercised this talent in lengthy requests, praise, thanksgiving and petition. In fact, during the first twenty years of his preaching career, the congregation was expected to stand during prayer time. This custom presented problems of physical endurance that were not remedied until the society voted on July 2, 1839, that the congregation be requested to sit during prayer time.

Outreach

Not long after arriving in Lima in 1819 to preach for the Lima Congregational Society, Rev. Barnard reached out beyond the local church to join the Ontario Presbytery. In 1706, the Presbyterians had organized their first Presbytery to govern local church congregations in Maryland, Delaware and Pennsylvania with New Jersey and New York following later. The new Presbytery grew so fast that it was transformed into the first Synod, which held its first meeting in 1718. Then in 1788, the Synod organized a General Assembly with four subordinate Synods in New York, New Jersey, Philadelphia, Virginia and the Carolinas. The first General Assembly met in the Second Presbyterian Church of Philadelphia in May 1789. Thus the basic governing organizations had been started years before Rev. Barnard came to Lima and with the growth in congregations there was a need for more Presbyteries and Synods. By 1800 there were 26 Presbyteries as compared with 16 some ten years before. In 1789, the year of the first assembly, there had been 419 churches as compared with 511 in 1803.

To understand why a Congregational pastor was able to join a Presbyterian organization, it is helpful to consider the following account of historical events. Cooperation between the Congregational and Presbyterian churches had been in effect since the adoption of the Plan of Union in 1800. This development reflected a spirit of interdenominational cooperation that lasted for 40 years. The Plan of Union made it possible for Congregational Churches to be connected with both Congregational and Presbyterian denominations. Presbyterian churches might be represented in the Congregational associations by their pastors and elders, while Congregational churches could be represented in the Presbyteries by pastors and committeemen. This arrangement made it possible for Rev. Barnard, a Congregational pastor, to attend meetings of the Ontario Presbytery. On February 4, 1820 he was elected the stated clerk of the Presbytery and that same year on May 21, 1820, the Lima Congregational Society joined the Ontario Presbytery and became fully Presbyterian. The main differences between the two denominations were in church government. The first election of elders by the Lima Presbyterian Society was on June 15, 1820, when the congregation chose Abel Bristol, Gordon W. Cook, Elijah Gifford and John Dixon. Nathan Rogers became the first deacon. The elders helped the minister oversee the spiritual life of the members. The deacon looked after the needs of the poor. The next addition to the elders was the election of G. Chamberlain on May 18, 1823. Following in 1827 two new elders were chosen to replace two resignations.

Trouble Within

From the time that Rev. Barnard had been hired for an annual salary of seven hundred dollars the Society had not been able to pay him the full amount. That they were beset with financial problems was shown in their renewed efforts to collect money from subscriptions for slips and pews for the pastor's salary. With the consent of the pastor, his yearly salary was adjusted to four hundred dollars a year, but the session minutes of 1825 show they even had trouble honoring this commitment and they continued to have trouble raising money to pay his salary during the late 1820s and early 1830s.

On July 3, 1827, the session had to deal with an entirely different problem. "In the early days of our country, extending through most of the nineteenth century, church discipline was expected and readily exercised as a duty of church officers."[26] The session minutes on that date show an example of the elders' control over behavior during worship services. Some unidentified persons (young people) had been defacing the pews on the west side of the gallery. They had used sharp edges to cut and mark the wood. Also, whispering and laughing during divine services described as immoral, indecent and disgraceful conduct needed to cease. A committee was named to ascertain the names of these young persons, that they might be reported to the proper authorities to put an end to such behavior. Bertha Cable's comments on church discipline outline the necessary steps taken to deal with offenders in the Rome church. This gives us a clue to how the elders dealt with the problem in Lima. The first step in Rome was as follows: "A complaint of wrong doing was brought to the attention of a board member who would then visit and talk with the accused, try to learn the truth of the matter and straighten it out."[27] It follows that, a designated elder, the equivalent of a board member in the Presbyterian Church, was considered the proper authority to visit the identified culprits and/or likely their parents to advise them that this kind of behavior would not be tolerated. Furthermore, the use of the words immoral, indecent and disgraceful to describe the guilty illustrate that these Puritan descendents had a strict and dignified no nonsense code of ethics in relation to behavior in church, where they went to worship God.

While John Barnard had been ministering to his church flock, he and his wife Ann had faced sorrow in their family with the death of their first son, John, who died when he was eleven days old. A second son, John F., was born in 1821 and third, Henry, was born in 1825. Blessed with a growing family, John's thoughts turned toward making a change in their living accommodations. This writer has been unable to determine where they stayed during their first seventeen years in Lima, but in the year 1826 John purchased from Asabel Warner a lot that became the site of his future home, not completed until ten years later.

A New Dwelling Place

After John Barnard purchased his lot, during the intervening years before construction began, he was busy not only with local responsibilities but also as clerk of the Presbytery and moderator of the Synod and attending yearly General Assembly meetings. Even so he managed to find time to decide to build a home for his wife and growing sons. Any or all of the following may have influenced his decision in favor of a cobblestone:

1. Having finished building locks and bridges for the Erie Canal in 1825, masons looking for other employment offered to build houses for settlers.

2. It is possible that while he lived in Rome he or his parents or both became acquainted with a mason, who came to the Lima area.

3. Cobblestone houses were constructed of easily available inexpensive materials.

4. Nearby limestone quarries were the source of lime, a necessary mortar ingredient.

5. Two other cobblestone houses were being built in Lima.

In addition to the reason why he made his decision to build a cobblestone house, there are many other unknowns in connection with the construction, the first being the date of the beginning of the work and who the workmen were. Since the date of the completion of the home was ten years after the purchase of the land, speculation about the exact schedule of events that led to the finished structure is not supported by recorded facts. It is logical to assume that excavation took hours of labor and laying the foundation added more. This part of the project could have taken months or even years. My sister and I recall having seen a date of 1832 in the basement, but the present owners are unable to find it. This led us to estimate the approximate time that Rev. Barnard was ready to acquire the stones needed for building the walls of the house was some time during or after 1832.

How did it happen that the needed stones were in plentiful supply? To answer this question, geologists conclude that the story began millions of years ago, unfolded through periods of geologic time, when change after change happened on the earth, during succeeding periods, that are classified and grouped into chronological eras. Geologists say that at one time a shallow inland sea covered most of New York state and the Great Lakes area west of the present Hudson river valley. Aquatic animals lived and died in this environment. Their remains sank to the bottom, forming layer upon layer of sediment. Subsequently, another series of geologic events included erosion of eastern ancient Appalachian Mountains causing additional layers of sand and clay adding additional weight and subjecting all to great pressure and the layers of sediment became limestone, dolomite, sandstone and shale. Finally, some 250 million years ago, as the salty sediment-filled sea dried up and the land mass emerged, new rivers began to cut into and expose our regional sedimentary bedrock.

The Cenozoic Era began millions of years ago, after all of the changes mentioned above, when layers of bedrock were being formed. It includes seven epochs, the last two being the Pleistocene or Ice Age and the Recent epoch, the former lasted one million years and the latter ten to twenty-five thousand years. During the Ice Age, glaciers covered large parts of North America and Europe several times, when great changes were made in the areas, where huge masses of ice moved slowly over the land, like the glacier that advanced southward from Labrador across Canada and into western New York. At this period in geological time the topography of this part of the state included hills and valleys that had been carved by the eroding action of streams and rivers, exposing bedrock. As it moved, the glacier broke off blocks of rock and pried others out of the ground. The moving ice rubbed these blocks against each other and scraped them against the bedrock over which it traveled. Imagine the tremendous power of this moving natural creation that not only transformed pieces of layered sandstone and limestone into smaller and smaller rocks but also collected, shaped, polished and transported southward stones that lay in its path. In addition, as it had traveled from its source in Labrador over Canada to New York, it brought samples of igneous and metamorphic rocks called erratics, because they did not originate from local bedrock. This explains why stones such as granite, gneiss and quartzite have appeared in local areas.

Eventually, when the climate warmed and the glacier began to melt, as it retreated it left deposits of debris, and an assortment of stones that had been tumbled and crushed along the way. The stones were of various kinds, sizes and shapes and have been named fieldstones. Also, other glacier-released stones were later smoothed and rounded by water tumbling action in lakes, rivers and streams that originated from glacial melt water. Thus, central and western New York remained from glacial time, a natural depository of resources that were useful for building, when the need arose starting with the settlement of the area by white men. In the beginning, the pioneers depended on felling local trees for constructing their homes, that with time evolved from log cabins to frame houses requiring sawed timbers.

A new development in residential construction began in western New York with the use of cobblestones for building homes. Truly, cobblestones are nature's gems, having been shaped, smoothed and polished by the natural lapidary forces that produced a plentiful supply of stones precious for building at a time, when it was expedient to use inexpensive material. The idea did not originate in this country, because many years before Europeans had used small stones in walls of dwellings. In our country some creative person started a trend that began approximately in 1825 and extended into the 1860's. Where and by whom the first structure appeared is not known. However, historians agree that the masons who worked on the Erie Canal had the skills and experience that could be applied to building houses. Not only had they used excavated sandstone and limestone for building canal locks, but also had made mortar from lime produced by crushing and burning limestone from local quarries. With the completion of the canal in 1825, many of the numerous masons that had migrated from New England or Pennsylvania to supply the demand for workers, bought farms and relocated in western New York.

Considering the evidence, it may be true that the first cobblestone building appeared on a farm owned by a mason retired from working on the Erie Canal. Faced with the need to plow and prepare his land for growing crops, he had to get rid of unwanted remnants of prehistoric time, the components of topsoil that hindered cultivation and growing. Some of these troublesome fieldstones became dry-stone-wall fences that separated parts of his farmland either for pastures or crop production. When he needed to build a home, he devised a method of using field cobbles to build the walls of his house, after he had used the larger fieldstones for the foundation. If he had children, they could have helped with the gathering and sorting according to size perhaps by dropping collected stones through a hole in a board. The definition of a cobblestone is one that can be held in the palm of one hand, supposedly that of an adult. Even so there would be differences, depending on the size of the hand, making the board screening more accurate and consistent, especially for the children who helped with the sorting.

To gain more knowledge of that first cobblestone building venture and its subsequent growth in an area centered in Rochester with expansion within 60 miles in all directions, including Lima, it is helpful to refer to Carl Schmidt's book *Cobblestone Masonry*. In this classic work he divided development into three periods, Early, Middle and Late. The Early Period extended from 1825 to 1835, the Middle Period from 1835 to 1845 and the Late Period from 1845 to the 1860s. Carl Schmidt examined what became known as the Barnard house and his description as it appears in his *Cobblestone Masonry* is as follows: "The cobblestones in the front wall are fieldstones of varied sizes, shapes and colors, although most of the stones are red sandstone. Scattered in the wall are also some round and oval lake-washed stones. They range from one and three quarters to two and one quarter in height and from three to six inches in length, laid four courses to a quoin height. Most of the cobblestones are about two by three and one-half inches. Horizontal joints are very wide, from one to one and one-half inches, and formed into straight 'V's, and the vertical joints are embellished with narrow 'V's. In the side wall the mason used larger fieldstones about three inches in height and from three to seven inches in length, with similar jointing. These are laid three courses to the quoin height. Corner quoins are fairly well squared sandstones, twelve inches high eighteen inches long and six inches thick. The four-inch thick window sills and nine-inch high lintels are made of red sandstone."[28]

It is significant to note that the Barnard house fieldstones, in size, color and shape, showed they had been carefully selected, as opposed to more random selection in the Early Period. Especially notable is the addition of a few lake-washed stones a characteristic typical of the early Middle Period and coinciding with the 1836 construction date of the Barnard cobblestone. During the late 1830's, water-rounded cobblestones appeared more frequently, and between 1840 and 1845 the rounded water washed cobblestones became the preferred material.

The original architectural features of late Federal/early Greek Revival style of the Barnard house remain today. These include the rectangular plan and the low-pitched gable roof. In addition, a semi-elliptical fan with wooden louvers and a stone surround with Keystone embellishes the front gable end. However, the Federal style of the street side front entry, as it was in Barnard's day, was changed in the late nineteenth century with the addition of Queen Anne double-doors and an encircling veranda, which much enhanced the appearance of the house. An account of the estimated sequence of these changes appears later in this narrative. The foregoing description applies to the house, before the Barnards sold it to future owners.

Cobblestones in the front wall

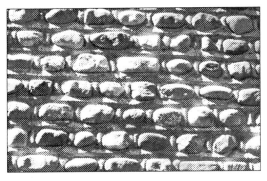

Field stones and lake washed stones

Window sills and lintels

Rectangular plan, low pitched gable roof and semi-elliptical fan

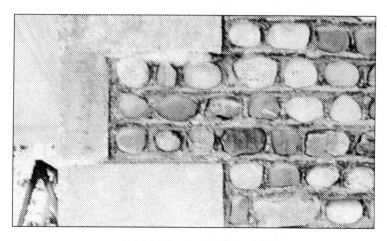

Cobblestones in side wall

1830s, 1840s and 1850s

Rev. Barnard's service in the larger church expanded when in 1828 he became clerk of the Synod and later moderator of the same in 1848. His participation in General Assembly meetings ceased in 1837, when he was disturbed by the disagreements over church government and doctrine that caused a split in this organization and led to the formation of two churches between the years 1837 and 1869, the Old School and the New School. The Old School was dissatisfied with the Plan of Union. Rev. Barnard, a peace loving person, refused to attend Assembly meetings during the years the church was divided and did not attend until the disagreements were resolved and the schools reunited in 1870 when he was eighty years old. Probably, influenced by his views, the Ontario Presbytery did not send representatives until 1852.

In conclusion, the governmental organization of the Presbyterian Church for both local and the district areas represented John Barnard's sphere of influence as follows:

1) The session included him and the ruling elders of his congregation.
2) The Presbytery consisted of elders and ministers from a limited district. It approved calls to ministers and installed them in local churches. Also, it had the authority to approve the purchase and sale of church property
3) The Synod covered a wider area, including a number of Presbyteries.
4) The General Assembly brought together representatives of every Presbytery once a year. It oversaw boards and agencies that conducted church functions.

At the end of 1836 bills had accumulated for the building of the house. The trustees' move to raise money to pay these bills resulted in selling at public auction 2 lots of land at the southeast corner of the church property. However, another building never occupied this site. Although the church contributed to the cost of construction, Rev. Barnard owned his home, never officially called the manse. From 1836 Rev. Barnard ministered for three more decades, not only presiding over the ruling affairs of his congregation and nurturing the spiritual lives of his church family but also continuing to be active in the Ontario Presbytery and the Synod.

The decade of the 1830s was an eventful time involving his ministerial duties as an adviser and a leader in winning new converts and applying the teachings of the Gospel to the lives of all who would be followers of Christ. In 1831, assisted by Rev. Norris Bull D.D. of Geneseo and Rev. A. E. Campbell of Pittsford, he conducted a 12-day revival that gained 160 new believers.

In 1832, deviating from the custom of the early Puritan worshippers and considering their comfort during services, the church members consented to allow a wood burning stove to heat the building. Before the end of the 30's decade the congregation approved several other noteworthy changes. On July 2, 1839 a committee was appointed to secure a change of the name of the Society from Charleston to Lima Congregational Society. By an act of the legislature the name of the town had been Lima since 1808. At that same meeting members voted to sit during prayer at public services and stand during singing. Again the need for comfort of the worshippers influenced their decision. Standing for their minister's lengthy prayers, sometimes 50 minutes, placed a strain on the stamina of the most robust, while it caused discomfort for the elderly or infirm, to say nothing about restless children. Rising for the singing was a welcome change of position from facing the pulpit, when they turned toward the opposite end of the sanctuary to face the choir. These same customs applied during the two services held on Sunday, one in the morning and one in the afternoon with Sunday school between. For those who brought their lunch their picnic ground was the graveyard next to the church.

The middle 1840s brought some changes and needed repairs to the sanctuary and the belfry. "On February 4, 1845 the Society resolved to make some improvements to the church by building a new desk, lowering the breastwork of the gallery taking out the slips above and putting in two rows of seats."[29] In the fall of the same year they hired Mr. Pierce of Mendon to repair the belfry.

Also in the 40's decade, Dr. Barnard's wise counseling helped to steer deliberations on the conduct of individual members, specifically adultery and stealing. Again he was a steadying influence, when it was questionable whether the house of worship should be used for reasons other than the worship of God. Slavery became a controversial issue and some wanted to meet in the church to discuss the problem. Also promoters of temperance wanted to hold meetings in the church building. Finally in 1847, with the trustees permission the building was opened for discussion of anti-slavery and other social issues. Largely, due to the skillful guidance of Dr. Barnard, there was no serious division in his congregation. Differences of opinion existed, but a peaceful coexistence prevailed under the leadership of a peace loving man.

The last years of Dr. Barnard's ministry in the 1850s began with a resolution passed to change the name of the society from The Charleston Congregational to the Lima Presbyterian Society to be effective in 1851. That same year "the society voted to raise $350 for the purpose of painting, repairing, insuring and putting blinds on the building. Also, Mr. Samuel Spencer was hired to grade the grounds in front of the church."[30] It is interesting that Lockwood L. Doty wrote in his book, *History of Livingston County,* "When the yard in front of the Presbyterian Church was graded, Indian skeletons were discovered by the hundred, as reported by those who then saw them."[31]

Only three years later, evidence of growth and prosperity was that the congregation had outgrown the building constructed in 1816 and were making plans to enlarge the church. They accomplished this by "cutting the church in twain, pushing the front part forward 20 ft. and enclosing the open space, at a cost of $2000."[32] Money was raised through subscriptions and the selling of land north of the carriage sheds. Seth Johnson bought the land and promptly gave it back to the church.

Evidence of favorable financial status had been reflected not only in the expansion of the church facility but also in the expenditures of the pastor in 1844 and 1854 to purchase two parcels of land that increased his holding to approximately seven acres at his home site on West Main Street, an acreage that continues to this day.

True to the saying that it takes more than bricks and mortar to make a house a home, the 1850 census showed that he and his wife Ann shared the comforts of their home with John's sister Abby and his 87-year-old father. Mary Oliver from England at the age of 14 was employed as a domestic to help with the household chores. Also listed this year, as a member of the family was their son Henry, a lawyer. In 1850, he married Lucina Williams. The couple moved to Indiana and then to Illinois. They had one daughter, Annie.

Sometime between 1850 and 1855 Rev. Barnard's father John senior died and in 1861 Henry died leaving his 38 year old widow Lucina and his daughter Annie, then 8 years old. Again, referring to the lines of "Bless This House" might John have uttered a similar prayer, "Bless this door that it may prove ever open to joy and love" and so with loving arms, he and his wife Ann invited their daughter-in-law and granddaughter to live with them.

Just 20 years after he had moved into his own home, at a time when membership had increased to 189 and the church had been stretched to accommodate increasing enrollment, the Presbytery of Ontario honored his request to retire as pastor of the Lima Presbyterian Society, after 38 years of service. Those with whom he had worked in the larger church lovingly and respectfully spoke of him as the "Beloved John." This gentle and loving spirit had blessed the people in his congregation and the community. So regretfully and sadly all of his associates respected his request to be relieved of his responsibilities. However, as we shall see, in his retirement he continued to be a caring and helpful person, always aware of the needs of others around him and willing to lend a hand. Desiring to know more about his home life, aside from his pastorate, I discovered an unexpected primary source of information, my Great Aunt's diary, which she wrote during the years 1865, 1866 and 1867. She was Martha Gillett, a sister of my grandfather, Schuyler Gillett.

Part II

Introduction

Let's turn back the pages of genealogy and flip forward to the time when the Gilletts and the Barnards were neighbors across the street from each other on West Main Street in Lima, N.Y. Tracing, as truly as possible, the growth of the family from the earliest known ancestor has evolved from writings about European and American history, from legal documents such as deeds and wills, from inscriptions on graveyard markers and from personal recollections. A host of people and other sources have contributed to what is known today.

Variations in the spelling of the family name have made accurate identification of descendents a challenging process. Through the generations the name has been spelled Gylot, Gylet, Galet, Galett, Gelot, Gilet, Gillet, Gillett, and Gillette. For example, genealogical researchers have concluded that the Huguenot, Rev. Jacques de Galett heads the list of known ancestors. He witnessed the Aug. 24, 1572 St. Bartholomew's Day massacre of Protestants in Paris and fled to Scotland, where he lived for fifty-seven years.

Protestant Reformation

A brief account of the events that led to that historic bloody purge in France begins with a German, Martin Luther, whose declarations in 1517 started the Protestant Reformation, which eventually spread from Germany to other European countries. In 1532, a young 23-year-old French law student, John Calvin, became converted to Protestant Christianity. In 1536 he published the first edition of his "Institutes of the Christian Religion." He established himself through more writings, as a second leader of the Protestant movement. John Calvin's doctrines on beliefs and church government greatly influenced the French Reformed Church. The name Huguenots applied to all French Protestants.

The rapid growth of the movement in France resulted in opposition from people with other beliefs. In 1559 there was an incident caused by conflicting religious convictions. "About 60 Huguenots were murdered in cold blood as they were going to church on Sunday in the little town of Vassy."[33] The intensity of the trouble increased when Catherine de Medici, mother of the ruling king, persuaded him to order the 1572 debacle in Paris, a tragedy that spread over France killing more than 30,000 Protestants. Thus, it is not surprising that Rev. Jacques de Galett, caught in the midst of the turmoil, decided to flee to Scotland, a land where the followers of John Calvin's teachings had been led by John Knox, a Scottish minister. Largely due to Knox's influence, the Scottish Parliament established the Presbyterian Church as the national church in 1560, twelve years before Jaques de Galett escaped to the country.

About 37 years after Jacques went to Scotland, his descendant Rev. William Gylett was instituted as Rector of Chaffcombe, Co. Simerset, England. He died April 2, 1641. According to his will, two daughters Habiah and Mary and three sons William, Jeremiah and Thomas were his beneficiaries. In addition it is highly probable that the elder William Gylett was the father of the two immigrant brothers Jonathan and Nathan, who had received their share before leaving England. Support for this conclusion is the opening statement of the will, which reads "My daughters, Habiah and Mary, land which my son Nathan made over to me by letter of attorney."[34]

As usual, moving forward with this family story is accompanied by looking backward to what happened some years before. In this case, recalling a part of England's history adds to continuity. In 1534, King Henry VIII "persuaded the Parliament to declare the English Church entirely independent of the Pope,"[35] but he was determined to keep the English Church true to Roman Catholic beliefs and customs in every other respect. This was one of the first signs that effects of the Protestant Reformation had reached England. Remember that Martin Luther's proclamations appeared in 1519. Under Henry VIII's son, the boy King Edward VI, "many mildly Protestant doctrines and practices were introduced and laid the foundation of the modern Episcopal and Anglican Church."[36] Under Edward's sister Mary, a loyal Roman Catholic, many Protestants left England to go to the continent, where the followers of Martin Luther and John Calvin were organizing churches. Protestant Elizabeth I succeeded Catholic Mary and reigned until 1603. She "rejected the Pope's rule over the English church,"[37] but retained much of the characteristics of the Roman Catholic Church. By this time, exiles, who had associated with Protestant believers on the continent, returned to their native land. Because they desired "to restore what they considered the 'purity' of the New Testament worship, they were called Puritans."[38] At first, they had no thought of leaving the Church of England, but envisioned changes within the existing church. During Elizabeth's rule Puritan ministers, who refused to follow the dictates of the national church were expelled from their pulpits or imprisoned. This was an example of persecution followed by more harsh treatment under the reign of James I, King of both England and Scotland, from 1603-1625. Following James' death, Charles I took the throne and ruled until 1647. He used even more drastic measures to deal with the Puritans. In 1628 a group of Puritans, 100 in all, left the shore of their homeland on the Mayflower and landed in Salem, Mass., where they settled and worshiped, as had been their custom in England. In 1630, 1,000 more Puritans sailed from England under the leadership of John Winthrop, who became the governor of their colony.

How all this religious turmoil had effected the lives of the Gillett ancestors is supported by few facts with much left to conjecture. It is safe to say that Rev. Jaques de Galett raised his family peacefully in Scotland, free to worship as a Protestant. Exactly when his son or grandson (the record is not clear whether Jacques was the father or grandfather of William) migrated to England and settled there is not known. However, we do know that William became rector in 1609 during the reign of James I. Apparently, he was not subject to persecution, because he was loyal to the Church of England. He lived in England until his death in 1641.

Emigration and Settlement

Conversely, the actions of his sons Jonathan and Nathan indicated they were attracted to the convictions of the Puritans and were willing to join a gathering of one hundred and fifty who prepared to leave England. People from three counties, Devonshire, Dorsetshire and Somersetshire, formed the group. Their pastors were "Revs. John Maverick and John Wareham."[39] The latter had been a well-known minister in Exiter, the capital of Devonshire County. Other notables were Mr. Ludlow and Mr. Rossiter, both magistrates and Mr. Wolcott, an able owner of a large estate. Members from Mr. Wareham's church and congregation included the Gillett brothers, Jonathan and Nathan. These venturesome converts, qualified with fortitude and faith, had a mission to accomplish, to have a part in extending the Reformation to a New World, because, to their satisfaction, the Puritan influence had been unable to "purify" the Anglican church of England. "On March 20, 1630, the company boarded the 'Mary and John', one of the first ships which came to New England in 1630 and arrived at Nantasket, May 30th."[40] "The next day the master of the ship left them on Nantasket point to shift for themselves. By the assistance of the old planters they proceeded up the Charles River to Watertown, but as they had many cattle and finding a neck of land at Mattapan, where there were good accommodations for them, they soon removed there and began a settlement which they named Dorchester."[41]

As early as 1631, the Dorchester inhabitants began to hear reports of conditions more favorable for farming in the fertile Connecticut River Valley. This news came from an Indian chief who visited the colonial governors to encourage them to send settlers to his area with assurance that "he would annually supply them with corn and give them 80 beaver skins."[42] The peaceful river tribes were being threatened by the warring Pequot Indians and the chief believed that an influx of English settlers could help to defend them. As a result of the chief's visit, Gov. Winslow, the governor of Plymouth, visited the area and encouraged building a trading house. The Dutch who had built a similar facility were potentially antagonistic to the English, but a peaceful settlement resolved the trouble.

Although Jonathan was willing to make his home in Dorchester, in 1634, he returned to England to marry Mary Dolbier (Dolbere) at Colyton in Dorchester county. The couple went back to New England, where their first son was born. Soon after Jonathan was made a freeman on May 6, 1635, a title bestowed when he became a landowner with holdings consisting of four and one-half acres. He had met property qualifications, had honorable personal qualities and was a member of the Congregational church, all of which entitled him to voting privileges in the governing of the town of Dorchester.

Destination Connecticut

In the year 1635, some of Mr. Wareham's congregation visited the Connecticut River Valley and were so impressed with what they saw that they returned to Dorchester to prepare to move their families. "On the 15th of October 1635, about 60 men, women and children with their horses, cattle and swine commenced their journey from Massachusetts through the wilderness to Connecticut. After a tedious and difficult journey through swamps and rivers over mountains and rough grounds, which were passed with great difficulty and fatigue, they arrived safely at the place of their respective destination."[43]

Mrs. Aldridge's account states that, with the Dorchester church and Rev. Mr. Wareham, Jonathan and Nathan removed about 1636 to Windsor, Connecticut. Also, she recorded that Jonathan and Mary had three children before they left Dorchester. Thus, all known information indicates that Jonathan and his family were not part of the first contingent that went from Dorchester to establish at Windsor. However, later immigrants must have faced many of the difficulties encountered by the 1635 travelers. In spite of the many conditions that made an easy journey impossible, Jonathan, his wife and three young children, Jonathan, Cornelius and Mary arrived at Windsor, "where Jonathan has a lot granted to him seventeen rods wide, near Mr. Wareham and across the Poquonnoc road from Alexander Alvord of the same company"[44]. Located near friends, whom they had known in England, they continued to live in Windsor. Whatever his source of income, presumably farming, it provided funds to purchase from Josiah Elisworth the Alexander Alfrod place, which remained in the family until 1866. Also, Nathan sold his Windsor Conn. property to his brother Jonathan. While his land holdings increased, his family grew with the addition of seven more children listed with their birth dates: Anna-1639, Joseph-1641, Samuel-1642, John-1644, Abigail-1646, Jeremiah-1647, and Josiah-1650.

The infant baptism of their children and the payment of six shillings for having the privilege to sit in the long seats in the church showed that religion was still an important part of their lives, nurtured by the leadership of the Rev. John Wareham, the first minister at Windsor. "He was about 40 years minister in New

England, six at Dorchester and 34 at Windsor. He was distinguished for his piety and the strictest morals, yet at times was subject to great gloominess and religious melancholy. Such were his doubts and fears, at some times, he administered the Lord's supper to his brethren and did not participate with them fearing that seals of the covenant did not belong to him. It is said that he was the first minister in New England who used notes in preaching, yet he was applauded by his hearers as one of the most animated and energetic preachers of his day. He was considered as one of the principal fathers and pillars of the church of Conn."[45] On April 1, 1670 death brought to closure the life of a man who had influenced the lives of many, including the Gillett brothers. He had a part in the inspiration and organization of the company that left England in 1630. He was with them on the tedious voyage to New England, remained their pastor in Dorchester, accompanied them on their perilous journey to Windsor and for thirty-four more years, guided his congregation in their application of Puritan beliefs. As his Windsor homestead was near Jonathan's, their families had been neighbors for many years. The following quote written after his death confirms that the Gilletts remained faithful members of the church that Rev. Wareham organized in Windsor. "Jonathan and his wife Mary were included in Matthew Grant's church list made thirty-seven years after the settlement (Windsor) of twenty-one members who were so in Dorchester and came up with Mr. Wareham and are still with us."[46]

The Colonists and the Indians

Inhabitants of Colonial Conn. could not escape exposure to relations between the colonists and Indians, the first New England generations of Gilletts being no exception. "In the early days of the settlement of Windsor settlers fear of Indian attacks made them seek refuge in a fortress at night with the protection of arms by their sides. They went to the fields in companies ready to defend themselves and it was common practice on the Lord's Day to go to meeting armed."[47] New England colonists feared the Pequot Indians of the Conn. River Valley more than any other Indians in the area. The peaceful tribes themselves feared the Pequots would force them from their lands. The warring tribes had migrated from the Hudson River Valley to neighboring Conn., where they had been responsible for attacking English traders. When the Puritans learned that the Pequots were plotting to drive the whites from Conn., they decided to take action. In 1637, the Conn. River towns mustered a company of 90 men, commanded by Capt. John Mason. Since it is known that Nathan was rewarded for his service in the Pequot War, it is reasonable to assume he joined the force that defeated the warring tribe with merciless tactics in two different locations. For his service in the Pequot War, Nathan was awarded 75 acres of land in Simsbury after 1640, when his name still appeared on a listing of Windsor residents.

The next noteworthy conflict between Colonists and the Indians occurred in the years 1675 and 1676 during King Philip's War, when trouble between the English and the Indians caused raids and massacres on both sides in Mass. and Conn. Philip, chief of the Wampaannoag Indians, claimed retaliation for unfair treatment of his two sons by the English. Determined to drive the white people from Conn., in June 1675, he led an attack on Swansea, Mass. and in the same year the Indians burned the town of Simsbury, Conn., located on land that originally belonged to the Indians, who sold it to the English settlers. Their settlement was called Massacoe, a part of Windsor. In 1670 a charter established it as a separate town and the name was changed to Simsbury. Five years later the town of Simsbury became involved in King Philip's War. The following quote from *Connecticut Historical Collections* describes the event as recorded by one who heard the story from those who were both witnesses and personal sufferers.

In the commencement of Philip's war in New England, in 1675 the town (Simsbury) was burnt by the Indians. Connected with which event, current tradition has preserved and handed down the following singular and extraordinary fact: that very shortly before this attack by the Indians, early one Sunday morning, as Lieut. Robe's father was walking the plain not far from his house, he very plainly and distinctly heard the report of a small arm, which much surprised him, it being the Sabbath. He found on returning to his house that his family also heard it. On going to the meeting at which the inhabitants from all parts of the town were assembled, it was ascertained that the report was heard at the same hour in every quarter. It was on further examination, found to have been heard as far south as Saybrook (50 miles) and as far north as Northfield, at that time the extent of the English settlements to the north. The report of this gun alarmed all Connecticut. The Governor summoned a council of war to meet at Hartford and the council issued an order for the inhabitants of Simsbury, one and all, immediately to withdraw themselves to Hartford, then the capital. This order was punctually obeyed. The fearful apprehension of being suddenly murdered by savages, put in motion and hastened along whole bands of women and children, with their men in the rear, with sheep, cattle and such utensils and conveniences as their short notice and hasty flight would permit. Hartford was twelve miles distant. Their heavy articles, such as pots, kettles and plough irons were secreted in the bottoms of swamps and wells.[48]

When the Indians entered the town, they found it deserted and proceeded to burn everything in sight. When the settlers returned to the desolate scene, they were faced with the task of rebuilding houses that had been reduced to ashes, so that a restored Simsbury would survive for future generations.

Belief that some of the Gilletts were directly affected by the burning of Simsbury is supported by the facts that Nathan had been awarded 75 acres in Simsbury for his service in the Pequot war and that he removed to Simsbury in 1670 five years before the start of King Philip's war. His wife died there in February, 1670. It is reasonable to assume that he was one of those who returned to rebuild. Further evidence to support his claim is that at least three generations of his descendents lived in Simsbury.

Windsor Residents

In the meantime, Nathan sold his Windsor property to his brother Jonathan who continued to reside in Windsor. Jonathan's family suffered from the tragedies of King Philip's war. Two of his sons died in military service. Joseph, age 34 was killed with Capt. Lothrop Sept. 16, 1675 at Battle Creek. Samuel, age 34, was killed in a battle with the Indians May 9, 1676 at Hatfield, Mass. Jonathan gave money to fund aid of sufferers by the Indian war at Simsbury and Springfield and was one of the committee of distribution. Soon after the end of King Philip's war, Jonathan died Aug. 23, 1677. His wife Mary Dolbier Gillett died Jan. 5, 1685.

Mrs. Bertha Aldridge compiled data about some of Jonathan and Mary's grown children, who they married, where they lived and birth dates of their sons and daughters. The members of Jonathan and Mary's family that are featured in her account are Jonathan, Cornelius, Joseph, John, Jeremiah and Josiah. In some cases, genealogical data continues beyond the first and second generations of Jonathan and Mary's descendents.

As this writer's story unfolds, it will become apparent that there is a special reason for learning as much as possible about Joseph and his descendents. Joseph was baptized on July 25, 1641 either in Windsor, Conn. or in Simsbury, Conn. (according to conflicting records). The Bertha Aldridge record states that Joseph married Elisabeth, daughter of John Hawks, had four sons and three daughters born 1664-1676. He bought the Hawks' place {in Windsor} and remained there until about 1673, when he moved to Deerfield, Mass. As one of the earliest settlers, he built on No. 32 on the Dr. Willard lot. On Sept.18, 1675, Joseph was killed in King Philip's War at Battle Creek. Following through several generations of Joseph's descendents leads to the birth of Moses Gillett in New Hartford, Conn. His parents were Matthew Gillett and Lois Douglas. Moses became the Yale graduate who supplied in the pulpit of the First Congregational (afterwards Presbyterian) church of Rome, N.Y. and was installed as pastor there Oct. 14, 1807. Eventually he was the mentor and friend of John Barnard, whose entry into the ministry has been described.

John, Mary and Their Descendants

Since Jonathan and Mary's son John was the forefather of my side of the Gillett family, tracing his descendents is of special interest. John was born at Windsor. There, on July 6, 1669, he married Mary Barber, daughter of Thomas and Jane Barber of Windsor and Simsbury.

The following extracts are from a publication entitled *The History of My Own Times* by Rev. Daniel Barber, A.M., printed at Washington in 1827. "My father's name was Daniel Barber. He was the son of Sergeant Thomas Barber, who was the grandson of Lieut. Thomas Barber, who commanded under Capt. Westover, in the first military company of said Simsbury. He was one of the original proprietors of that township, as appears from his name being still on the original charter."[49] According to this quotation, Mary Barber who married John Gillett was Lieut. Thomas Barber's daughter. In Windsor John Gillett bought Joseph Phelp's place and probably lived there in Windsor. He and Mary had four sons and one daughter before he died in Simsbury at the young age of 38 leaving his wife, a widowed mother of 5 children, John 9 years, Samuel 5 years, Thomas 4 years, Benjamin I, 2 years, Mercy 10-11 months. The widow Mary married Capt. George Norton and lived with him in Suffield, where they were among some of the early settlers. At first the town was part of Mass., having been bought from two Indian chiefs for about the equivalent of 100 dollars. With the issuing of a grant in 1670 for becoming a town, it was in the early stages of development, when Mary and the stepfather of her children began to raise their family there in 1682. The 2 year old Benjamin, destined to be the first of three by the same name, grew up in Suffield and in 1705 married Elizabeth Austin and had 9 children one of whom was Benjamin II, born in Suffield in 1708. Benjamin II married Lydia Hayes and had 14 children, including Benjamin III; the last of the Gilletts to be born before Suffield became part of Conn. in 1752. Benjamin III and his wife Abigail Austin had 11 offspring, at least seven born in Suffield, 2 in Salisbury and 2 with unknown birthplaces.

Using the data known today, it is possible to conclude that Alexander, son of Benjamin III, and his wife Sarah migrated to New York state from Connecticut sometime before 1805, because there is definite proof that John, their second child, was born in this state. Tracing the exact location of John's birth and that of the following children is somewhat nebulous due to the changing of county lines in the early 1800s. Seneca County went through a series of changes between the dates of 1804 and 1829 According to the New York state census, the Gilletts lived in Romulus in 1810, and in Junius in 1820, both part of Seneca County. The birth dates of their nine children indicate that eight of their children were born in Seneca County before the 1829 change. Alexander and Sarah's children and their birth dates were:

Polly, February 3, 1803	Benjamin, May 28, 1816
John, May 5, 1805	Terry, June 8, 1821
Asa, May 19, 1807	Lydia, September 8, 1823
Nathan, May 19, 1807	Luther, June 22, 1827
Sarah, August 19, 1813	

After the Gilletts had been living in Seneca County for at least fourteen years, the Liddiard family came from England and located on a farm near Waterloo, which was part of Junius township at that time. The names of the Liddiard children and their birth dates were as follows:

Charlot, April 25, 1794	Sarah, April 5, 1806
John, Aug. 27, 1798	Dinah, Sept. 18, 1808
Mary, Oct. 8, 1801	Martha, May 19, 1810
William, Oct. 23, 1803	Elizabeth, Mar. 5, 1812
Ann, Mar. 29, 1805	Thomas, June 17, 1815

It is of special interest for future developments to note the ages of Martha and Ann. All of the children were born in England, before the family came to New York State in 1819.

Exactly how and where the Gilletts and the Liddiards became acquainted is not known. We do know that a very few years after they came to this country, the Liddiards moved to Geneva, occupying a house on Milton Street. In spite of not being able to add more details, other than the proximity of Junius township and Waterloo, somehow, John Gillett and Martha Liddiard had met and were married on Oct. 5, 1826 by Rev. Orin Clark, when John was twenty-one and Martha was sixteen. Eventually, they bought property in Lima, N.Y. and continued to live there.

Land Purchase in Lima

Verification of the fact that the Gilletts became Lima landowners in 1833 is provided by their deed to West Main Street property purchased on March 22, 1833 by Asa and John Gillett from Jonas Humphrey and his wife Eunice for a sum of six hundred dollars. A quote from the deed is as follows: "Beginning on the north side of the state road at the southwest corner of the lot which stands the Methodist Episcopal Church," henceforth described by surveyors measurements in degrees and rods for distances north, west and south "to the north side of said road thence easterly along said road five rods and seventeen links to the place of beginning containing one acre and thirty-one and three fourth rods of land being the same premises of which the said Jonas Humphrey now resides and which was conveyed to him by Frederick House and Prudence his wife by deed dated 5th day of October, AD 1828."

A second deed made on March 14, 1836 between Asa Gillett and Lucy his wife and John Gillett, for a sum of five hundred and thirty-five dollars, sold their half share of the property to John and Martha Gillett, thus making them sole owners of the same property purchased by the two brothers in 1833.

According to the first deed, it is significant to note that the previous owners of the Gillett land purchase, Humphrey and House, are names that appear in the history of the first Methodist Episcopal Church in Lima as recorded in the *History of Livingston County* by Smith and Cole in 1881. They wrote, "During the year 1827, Rev. Micah Seager, then preacher in charge on the Bloomfield circuit, preached here (Lima) occasionally for at that time Methodism had not assumed organized form in this locality."[50] In the autumn of 1827 Rev. John Parker, then stationed at Norton's Mills (now Honeoye Falls), was invited to hold regular services in the Town Hall of Lima. Under his ministry a powerful revival was enjoyed, the influence of which thoroughly permeated the community and resulted in the organization of the Methodist Episcopal Church at "Lima Corners." The Rev. John Parker organized the society in March 1828. Among the original members of the society were Frederick House and Eunice Humphrey. (Note that in the preceding paragraph Frederick House sold his property to Jonas Humphrey in October of the same year 1828.) The membership rapidly increased, the Town Hall soon became too small to accommodate the congregation, and the creation of a church edifice was soon begun and completed in a few months. It is reasonable to assume that when Frederick Humphrey bought the property adjacent to the Methodist Episcopal Church, the building had been finished or was near completion. "This humble edifice was long the crowning glory of the hillside on the street leading toward Avon,"[51] an established claim to distinction, when the Gillett brothers purchased the adjoining property in 1833.

Only three years prior to the Gilletts' arrival in Lima the Genesee Conference of the Methodist Church had selected Lima as the site for an educational institution that was founded in the summer of 1830 as the Genesee Wesleyan Seminary. Erection of the first building occurred in 1832 for a school destined to be the seat of learning in Livingston County. The attendance that first year was 230 gentlemen and 11 ladies.

Why did the Gillett brothers decide to invest $600 dollars in land and a house in Lima on a route that had evolved from an Indian foot path, to a trail, to a road, the latter designation authorized by legislation as early as 1794? This year brought improvement to the route from Old Fort Schuyler, now Utica, through Canandaigua to the Genesee River, and in the year 1809 a road was established between the Hudson and the Niagara Rivers. It follows that the question of how the brothers came is easier to answer than why they came. Since they had lived east of Lima, their migration westward followed a route that had been used by many early settlers, who had traveled from east to west before 1833, among them Rev. John Barnard, who made the trip from Rome to Lima in 1819. Lima had been a stagecoach stop, the route having been established sometime before 1793, and mail had been carried over this road on horseback as early as 1798.

Clues as to why the brothers chose Lima may depend on conditions that existed there at the time of their arrival. Its situation on the road used by pioneers and immigrants had made a need for building inns and taverns to accommodate the travelers. Taverns and inns were built about a mile apart from Canandaigua to the Genesee River, seven within the limits of Lima, all doing a flourishing business during the first part of the 19th century. There were stores where people could purchase general merchandise and some food staples: salt, pepper, sugar, tea, spices, etc. One general merchant was Grout with his partner E.A. Sumner in partnership until 1836. Another merchant was J. Franklin Peck who began business about 1833. He was burned out in 1835, rebuilt and continued his business until about 1840. There were two mills, a gristmill and a sawmill, and a brickyard that had produced building material for houses already in existence.

Parents in Lima for years before the Gilletts came had shown a concern for the education of their children. In 1797 there were three commissioners of Common Schools, elected by the town meeting to apportion to the school districts their share of public money and at that time there was $60.40 due for support of a common school. As previously recorded in Part 1 of this account, local residents under the leadership of the Charleston Congregational Society had supported the building of a combination schoolhouse, town hall and a house of worship, completed in 1804. Subsequently the worshippers went to their new church in 1818, but the original brick building continued to be the schoolhouse until it was replaced in 1860.

So, for a combination of reasons including the attractiveness of the town and other unknown personal convictions, the Gilletts settled in a town that has been home for many generations of their descendents.

At Home on West Main Street

John Gillett and Martha Liddiard were married in Geneva October 5, 1826 by Rev. Orin Clark. Before they moved to Lima they had two children born in Ontario County: a son, George P., born in 1831 and a daughter, Mary J., born in 1832. Soon after their move, a second daughter Martha S. joined the family living in a house directly across the street from the property owned by

Rev. John Barnard, whose cobblestone house was being constructed and was completed in 1836, one year before the birth of the Gilletts' third daughter, Lucy, in 1837. Their family continued to grow with the birth of their fourth daughter, Elizabeth H., in 1839. The second son, George, came in 1842, the fifth daughter, Amanda M., came in 1844, the sixth girl, Frances A., in 1847, and finally the third son, Schuyler L., was born in 1849.

I have a limited amount of information about the growing years of John and Martha's family. However, it is safe to assume that some of the children's elementary education was in the original red brick schoolhouse erected in 1804 on the site of the present Town Hall. From 1797 public money had been appropriated for school districts. In 1827 the several school districts had been organized in the town and boundaries of each established in the year. In the year 1824, the Gilletts' district, No. 9, received $33.28 for 88 pupils, and another district had 5 pupils and received $1.89. The money was expended in paying teachers duly qualified by law. Through the years, District No. 9, comprising the village and some outlying territory, had the largest apportionment. Since the red brick schoolhouse was replaced in 1860, all of the Gillett children had not completed their elementary education by that date. The census for the year 1860 taken in July shows that all the family was at home except for the oldest daughter Mary. At that time John was 55, his occupation a butcher, Martha, his wife, was 50, George 29, Martha S. 26, occupation a teacher, Lucy 23, Elizabeth 21, Amanda 16, Frances 13, Schuyler 11. The three youngest children had attended school within the year, probably in the red brick schoolhouse, which was torn down and another building was erected on the same site, but further back from the road than the first one. This new schoolhouse was a two-room, one story brick building with two teachers employed. It is likely that at least the two youngest children continued their education there.

In addition to suppositions about the childrens' education, a second assumption is that the conveniently located Methodist

Episcopal church next door became the center of the family's religious life. This conclusion is supported by entries in Aunt Martha's diary that the family showed faithful attendance in the M.E. Church during the years 1865, 1866, and 1867. The proximity of the original church next door on West Main Street lasted until 1843, when the building was moved to a new location on Rochester St. Three Gillett children were born after that date.

The Gillett family was destined to cope with many sad events. The first of them was the death of their three-year-old son in 1845. It is unfortunate that my knowledge of family affairs in their early Lima years is limited basically to births and deaths. George, the eldest son died in 1860, age 29. Then in 1863 the family endured the sorrow of losing to death three more family members. The first was Mary who died May 6 at the age of 31. She had married and did not live at home. On May 23 Amanda died at the age of 19 and on June 1st the dear mother of this maturing family was fatally burned when her dress caught fire while she was cooking before an open fireplace. It has been told that she died of suffocation. This left the eldest surviving daughter, 30 year old Martha, to assume the role of mother to care for her father, her sisters, Lucy 26, Elizabeth 24, Frances 16 and her brother Schuyler age 14. I have Aunt Martha's diary which she wrote beginning in the year 1865, two years after her Mother's death, and continued through 1867.

The Diary

As an introduction to the contents of the diary, it is helpful to review some of the events that had been happening in Lima between the dates 1833 and 1865. Outstanding was the growth of Genesee Wesleyan Seminary, including the addition of Genesee College. In 1842, the first building of the Seminary burned without loss of life, library books or equipment. It was replaced in 1844 by a 4 story high edifice with 100 rooms. Later, verandas were added to embellish the structure. Also, a boy's dormitory was built on the west side of the campus. In 1849 Genesee College was founded and in 1850 College Hall was built. The two institutions were operated under one management and a joint Board of Trustees for 20 years, and in 1854 the total enrollment of students reached 1058.

In addition to the Methodist Episcopal and Presbyterian churches existing in 1833, 2 more congregations built churches. In 1848 the first attempt to organize a Catholic church was made by Father O'Connor from Canandaigua. At that time there were only 8 or 9 Catholic families in Lima, and of those 8 or 9 families there were no more than 15 persons able to contribute to a building fund. However, this small number donated the sum of $350. The land for the church was given by Tom Yorks, for $35, and he also supervised the building of the little church and worked on its construction, which was completed in 1849, on the ground where the rectory now stands.

Although the Baptists had been meeting as early as 1834 and they had written their "Articles of Faith", in 1854, they chose a meeting place near the center of the village of Lima and 15 members organized the Lima Baptist Church. Their house of worship was erected and completed in 1856.

For the sake of continuity a brief history of some of Lima's other developments will accompany diary entries that describe daily activities, such as going to the store, to the burying ground, to the Post Office, the arrival of the stage, etc.

Aunt Martha's diary is a treasure of information about family life in the middle of the 19th century, the necessary chores that kept them clean and nourished and dressed in the style of the day, their social and religious life and, in addition much about Lima, New York, that had emerged from pioneer days to a growing community. Writings for the years 1865 and 1866 are contained in little leather bound volumes 2" by 4" that have three daily entries to a page. The 1867 volume is the same size but in some cases a daily entry occupies a single page.

Gillett family portrait taken sometime before George died in 1860. First row left to right: Martha, Mother Martha, John, Schuyler Back row: Frances, Lucy, George, Mary, Elizabeth, Amanda

Martha Gillett began her account of each day with a weather report. Her favorite descriptive word was pleasant or variations from not pleasant, unpleasant, very pleasant, quite pleasant, rather pleasant, middling pleasant, to tolerably pleasant or pleasant and thawing, pleasant most of the time, pleasant and warm. No matter what season, winter, spring, summer or fall, that word appeared, not everyday but often. She recorded the temperature, especially on the coldest days in terms of mercury readings. For example on Friday, Jan. 20, 1865 the mercury was 9° above at 9 A.M. Sometimes she simply recorded the degrees omitting the word mercury. Some days she described the weather in one or two words; other times she might use 6 or 7 or more. On Sunday March 12, "Very cold night, froze in the kitchen." Wednesday March 15, "warm and pleasant, heard the first robin." Saturday March 18, "Wind blew dreadfully through the night." In the three years that she kept a diary she wrote about 1,090 weather reports, making note of snow, wind, rain, thunderstorms, etc. She was an amateur meteorologist, not qualified to make predictions like our

TV specialists; nevertheless her daily recordings have stood the test of time and are still readable.

According to the diary, the year 1865 brought several events that deserve special mention. The first of them concerns her sister Frances (Frank or Frankie) who was 18 years old. On February 1 a foreboding came when Lib and Martha went downtown and paid for an inhaling tube. She wrote on February 2, Frank and self went riding. (Apparently that was something they did when someone was not feeling well.) Also, that same day she cut sleeves for Frank's nightdress. Feb. 9: Father went to Dr. Gibson who sent a prescription. Feb. 10: Dr. Gibson came to see Frank. Thurs. Feb.16: Dr. Gibson came again. Feb. 17: Frankie's bed put up in the back room. Sat. Feb. 18: Watched Frankie last night. Ella Mosher sent Frankie an orange. Feb. 23: Julie Scovill watched with Frank last night. Other friends brought Frankie oranges and grapes. Mon. Feb. 27: About 10 friends came to call among them Miss Abbie Barnard (Rev. Barnard's sister). Feb. 28: Dr. Barnard one of the callers. March 1: Abbie Barnard & Dr. Barnard & Dr. Gibson among others were present when Frankie died near nine P.M. She was 18 years, 9 months and 7 days old. She was laid out by Mrs. Arnold & Mrs. Barnard, Dr. Barnard's wife. Thurs. Mar. 2: A great many called. Mar. 3: two friends brought a wreath and flowers. Sat. Mar. 4: Very stormy. Frankie's funeral held at the house at 10 A.M. Bro Kellogg officiated (M. E. pastor). Large attendance. Mrs. Barnard and Mrs. Salmon (next door neighbor) here for dinner. She listed the bearers and the pallbearers. This day-by-day account speaks for itself. The illness, death and funeral all happened within the walls of their house. God's presence was there in the persons of a loving family, the faithful pastor, the doctor who made house calls, the good friend and loving neighbor Dr. Barnard, his wife and his sister and many other devoted friends. It could be said that in the presence of illness and death, God truly did "Bless This House."

The second series of noteworthy events recorded by Aunt Martha in 1865 were related to the progress of the Civil War and the reaction of Lima residents to news that caused celebration. On Monday, April 3, 1965, Lima's people learned that Richmond been taken. "In Virginia, Grant at last achieved his goal. In April 1865, he turned Lee's right flank and seized the railroads supplying Richmond. The Confederate troops had to evacuate Petersburg and Richmond."[52] On Tues. April 4, 1865 Aunt Martha wrote "Pleasant till night then it rained. Mrs. H. Landon here to tea, Phebe called. Town meeting, Bells rang, Cannon fired, drums beat and a general jubilee till after midnight." Then on Monday, April 10 she wrote: "drizzling sort of day. Lucy and I washed. Exciting news, Cannons roared, speeches made, torch light procession, bells rang. All the corner illuminated. Lucy called at Dr. Barnard's". The historic meeting of Grant and Lee at Appomattox, where Lee surrendered, had occurred on Sunday April 9, the day before Lima's celebration.

"On the evening of April 14, 1865, Lincoln attended a performance of 'Our American Cousin' at Ford's theater in Washington. A few minutes after 10 o'clock a shot rang through the crowded house. John Wilkes Booth, one of the best-known actors of the day, shot the President in the head from the rear of the Presidential box. Lincoln was carried unconscious to a neighboring house. He died at 7:22 A.M. on April 15."[53] On Saturday, April 15 Martha wrote, "Abraham Lincoln died" and on Sunday, April 16: "Union meeting in the forenoon at M. E. church occasioned by the death of Abraham Lincoln. Speeches by different persons."

Martha made one more entry on Monday, May 15, about the Civil War: "News of Jeff Davis capture." When the news of Appomattox reached North Carolina, Johnston surrendered to Sherman on April 26 near Durham. President of the Confederacy, Jefferson Davis fled southward and was captured in Georgia. One wonders how news from the outside world reached Lima. The stagecoach daily delivered not only passengers but also mail and news from other parts of the country.

Reading the diary for the first time, I discovered that on Saturday, May 13, 1865 Martha and Lib (Elizabeth 26) went to see Dr. Gibson and that same day Mrs. Barnard brought Libbie some fish and two days later she brought Lib asparagus. This made me suspicious that Lib was not well, especially when I read that Miss Abby (Dr. Barnard's sister) brought more asparagus to Libbie on another day. As I had noticed, when their sister Frankie became ill, friends began to bring food to her. During the month of June, Martha and Lib went riding once nearly every day and toward the last of the month they went twice a day. Then I was sorry to read the entry on Thursday, June 21 as follows: "A very hot day. Libbie and I rode out in the morning. Lucina (Dr. Barnard's daughter-in-law) & Mrs. Warner called. Libbie sat at the dinner and tea table for the last time." On the next day: "Cooler, Libbie and I rode out." Martha wrote the names of 12 people who came to call, then on Saturday, July 1st: "Pleasant. Dr. Barnard here, talked and prayed. Mrs. Barnard, Addie Yorks, Frankie Kellogg here to sit for a while. Mrs. Beadle & Mrs. Galentine called. Libbie died between 11 and 12 o'clock P.M. She was 26. Mrs. Barnard and Mrs. Winams laid her out. Sunday: "Some rain cool. Libbie lies a corpse on the sofa. A great many here." Monday, July 3rd: "Pleasant. Libbie's funeral at 2 P.M. Mr. Kellogg made remarks." Martha listed the bearers and the pall-bearers. As was the case when Frankie died, there was no mention of the grief that overwhelmed this family, having witnessed the death of three members in 1863 and two more in 1865, but Martha did faithfully record the names of many who were with the family during Libbie's last days and the funeral. This was Martha's way of paying tribute to the ones who showed their love by their sympathetic presence. Again God had blessed this house with loving friends of "all the folk who dwelt within."

Activities

Having referred to the highlights of the year 1865, my intention now is to give an overview of diary entries by grouping them under subject headings such as weather reports, food preparation, cleaning and seasonal maintenance, sewing, transportation and travel, holidays, Father's business, etc. To avoid needless repetition of routine daily and weekly chores, the following condensation shows how an industrious family provided for their needs steadily and consistently.

Monday was time for washing and drying. Clothes were hung outside to dry. On July 31, 1865, Martha tried the wringer for the very first time. On October 16, she washed clothes in the washer. In 1866, there are references to Father machining the clothes for her. Without a doubt, the equipment was hand operated. On Tuesday they ironed, but quite often this task might require more than one day to finish, especially when starching of some things was part of the process. Work on Wednesday, Thursday and Friday included sewing, baking, churning and cleaning. Usually Saturday was a day for baking (perhaps bread, pies and cake). Also, some cleaning, like mopping, might be done. Any time left after the completion of regular daily tasks could be put to varied uses. For example, on Tuesday, January 17, she wrote: "Very cold. Rinsed up clothes, baked bread, churned. Mr. Kellogg called in the morning. Schuyler took me downtown and back, after tea finished my hood." Monday, February 13 was a rare exception. "No washing today. Lib baked cake. Edie Arnold came after sweet milk. Father went to Honeoye after medicine." Then she said she wrote two letters. Tuesday, February 14: "Very pleasant. Washed on the next day, hung out clothes and on Thursday Lib and Martha ironed, baked bread and so on."

Food Preparation

After the deaths of Frankie and Libbie, the family members totaled 5, John, the father, Ann, his second wife whom he had married in 1864 (she was his first wife's sister), Martha, Lucy and Schuyler, all usually home for meals. The diary for 1865 and 1866 does not give much information about mealtimes and exact menus. However, in 1867, Martha used more page space for writing about days' events. It was here I learned that breakfast, which Lucy usually prepared, was at 7 A.M. At no time did Martha ever say what they ate for the first meal of the day. Certainly, following the meal, there were dishes to be washed, milk to be skimmed (the beginning of butter making), beds to be made and other chamber work to be done. These were just some of the chores that needed to be finished before or during the preparation of dinner, usually the midday meal. What they may have eaten for dinner was learned from references to food preparation such as cooking meat for mince pie with other meat for dinner; picking a chicken or duck; using venison that Henry sent; peeling potatoes; paring apples for sauce; cooking onions, squash and greens; picking peas and berries; and gifts of asparagus from the Barnards. The supply of home canned or preserved food was replenished depending upon what was in season. Produce preserved included tomatoes, pears, peaches, grapes, strawberries, currants, quinces, plums and pickles.

The diary may not have had much information on mealtimes but it has plenty of details about baking and baked goods on an almost daily basis. The baked goods that came from the Gillett oven were eaten with a meal as tasty treats for dessert or were enjoyed at teatime. Bread was made twice a week, most often on Tuesdays and Saturdays. However, there were times when this weekly routine changed, as was mentioned before. Yeast, a necessary ingredient in bread dough, was cultured at home in those days. When Aunt Martha mentioned yeast making she did not describe the procedure. She probably prepared a batter of flour, potato water, salt and sugar and left it sitting uncovered for several hours. Yeast cells in the air entered the batter, grew and reproduced. How yeast worked in bread dough is the same today, when we have the advantage of using store bought yeast. Enzymes from the yeast cells convert the starch in the flour to sugar. The sugar is then changed to alcohol and carbon dioxide gas. The gas bubbles up through the mixture, forming the familiar bubbles in bread dough, making the mass light and porous. When the bread is baked, the alcohol evaporates and the yeast plants are destroyed.

Desserts in the Gillett household were plentiful and varied. On Saturdays, Martha regularly baked pies and cake, in addition to bread, but baking on more than one day a week was necessary to supply the need for cookies and other goodies. Although there was no baking involved in making fried cakes, she made them often too. Biscuits can be added to the list and rarely even crackers.

Whether she used butter in baking I do not know, but it is more certain that she used lard, especially to make piecrust. Preparation of both types of shortening was a regular procedure usually not on the same day. Separating the cream from the milk was done by skimming almost daily. They churned on Tuesday and worked the butter on Wednesday. Very likely part of her churning equipment was a dasher, a wooden stick with a round blunt end like that of a wooden potato masher. The dasher was plunged up and down in the earthenware churn until butter formed. The churn and dasher for butter making was a household necessity throughout the 1800s. When the butter separated from the cream, it was gathered into a mass and the liquid drained off. Then it was worked with a ladle by pressing and squeezing. Cold water was added along with sprinkles of salt and the butter was set in a cool place to harden. Then it was worked and kneaded until not a drop of water exuded and the butter was perfectly smooth and close in texture and polish and made into shapes. It is not surprising butter making was a process that required two days to complete.

Trying lard was a simpler process that involved cutting pieces of hog fat into a pan and heating them until the fat melted. The resulting liquid was strained to remove pieces of flesh or tissue and cooled in a container ready for use. On Tuesday, February 7, she mentioned trying lard and churning. The next time she wrote about trying lard was April 22. On the other hand in that same time period she had churned and worked butter many times.

Cleaning

If the mop and broom were symbols of cleanliness, then the Gilletts were very clean, because they used them often, daily or weekly with more thorough procedures on a seasonal basis. They swept the carpeted rooms and mopped the floor of the cook room regularly, doing the latter on Saturday, but more often as needed. Aunt Martha did not have the luxury of a carpet sweeper, which was not invented until 1876 or a vacuum cleaner used first in 1899. Martha's notations about seasonal cleaning in 1865 occurred during the months of April and May, when she and Lucy did five rooms upstairs. Aunt Martha did her bedroom and closet. Downstairs they cleaned the front and back parlors, the dining room, the pantry and the cook room, a total of eleven rooms not counting closets. The fall cleaning started in September and was more or less a repeat of what they had done in the spring with the added chore of cleaning the coal burning stoves in preparation for winter. The activity extended into the month of December, when they took up the dining room carpet, cleaned the floor and the cupboards, washed windows and washed and ironed curtains.

In 1866 seasonal activity started in January, when they blackened the cook stove and cleaned the cellar. On February 1st they swept most of the rooms in the house and fixed the front room pipes. In the spring they cleaned Lucy's room and papered it. They took up Martha's carpet and Father white washed in her room. They papered the front chamber. In April Martha varnished ten chairs, cleaned and varnished other furniture. On May 3rd she took up the back parlor carpet and commenced repairing it. On May 4th they were papering the back parlor and blackening the stove. On May 5th they mopped and painted the back parlor. On May 7th they put down the back parlor carpet. Tuesday, May 8th: "Took up carpet, washed paint, scraped paper off the wall in the dining room. Father white washed and I washed the ceiling. Varnished the secretary." May 9th: "Papered the dining room."

In the spring of 1867 they did the usual cleaning, but this time she wrote about washing carpets. On May 11th: "Moved the dining room stove and cleaned the chimney." May 30th: "Cleaned the pantry and white washed the cook room."

The use of white wash in the house has been somewhat of a puzzle, since we think of white wash being used to coat barn walls and fences. Aunt Martha did not tell how they made their white wash, but most likely it was composed of lime, possibly flour, whiting, salt, water and glue. An accepted fact is that white wash coats surfaces with an alkaline layer that discourages the growth of bacteria. It would make sense that the Gilletts used it as a type of disinfectant. In addition, it is credited with being a sealer that can smooth rough surfaces, perhaps before painting or papering. In more than one instance, Father white washed after the rug had been taken up, making one wonder if he white washed the floor. Aunt Martha simply wrote Father white washed but did not specify what he white washed. One exception is the entry where she wrote they white washed the cook room, which obviously had plastered walls that were not painted or papered. The best conclusion is that the Gilletts used white wash on a variety of surfaces including wood trim, floors and walls.

Sewing

Sewing was an important and necessary part of providing for the family. Aunt Martha was the main seamstress, but Lucy and Aunt Ann did some sewing too. In the year 1865, Martha's role as older sister and mother to her 16 year old brother is especially obvious in her making sure he had the clothes he needed. During that time she made him three pairs of pants, at least two of them lined, a coat, a vest, a collar and a waist. For her sister Lucy she pleated a dress skirt and made a dress, for Frankie a nightdress. For herself she made a thin dress, and she fixed her bombazine dress and put a band on her bombazine dress skirt. Bombazine is a twilled fabric of which the warp is silk and the weft is worsted cotton, much used for mourning garments. She surely had need for this type of dress, having mourned for five members of her own family.

Other dress materials unfamiliar to me were commonly used. One was delaine. On October 25 she was sewing on a seeded delaine dress. Delaine was a lightweight fabric, originally of wool and later a combination of cotton and wool. On April 28, 1865 she put a band on a balmoral skirt. This cloth was a heavy serviceable striped or figured woolen fabric. Women made a balmoral skirt or petticoat to wear under a skirt. Who knows whether polyester and denim will be worn 100 years from now and if not, what kind of materials will replace them?

Cloaks and capes for outdoor wear were fashionable in those days as were hoods and bonnets, which Lucy and Martha made. On October 4 she wrote, "I went to Frankie Warner's and had my cloak cut out." Two years later on October 7, 1867 Martha wrote, "Lucy and I made our white merino capes", finery that they likely wore to Miss Abba Northrop's wedding the next day. Merino was a soft woolen cloth made of the wool from Merino sheep, one of a hardy breed with long fine silky wool, originally from Spain. Merino wool is still used today for fine woolen garments.

On November 10, 1865 she wrote, "Mrs. Long cut and fitted my basquene." On November 11 she was sewing on her basquene and on November 15 she finished it. I am not sure how to interpret her diary entry. According to definitions there are two words, basque and basquine. Her spelling replaces the i with an e. The definition of basque is a woman's blouse with a tight fitting waist, made with or without a short skirt attached. Basquine is an elaborate outer garment worn by Basque women. Since Aunt Martha's basquene required fitting, her description is more like the word Basque than Basquene, however the use of the word probably depended on the terminology used 139 years ago.

Study of the family portrait taken in 1860 or before reveals a lot about what the family wore, when they were clad in their best, having been made by nimble fingers using cloth and a needle and thread. It is obvious that detachable cuffs and collars were fashionable and practical, because they could be washed separately. Aunt Martha mentioned making many of them especially for Schuyler, her sister and herself. February 7, 1867: "Stitched and made 10 buttonholes in cuffs." They supplied a decorative touch to the dark fabrics, as did the braids, stripes and bands used for trimming.

In addition to outer garments their underwear was also homemade. Martha wrote several times about making chimeses. Her spelling was chimese, as opposed to chemise, as a loose, skirt like undergarment worn by women and girls. Martha even spent extra time embroidering the yokes and bands of her chimeses. According to the custom of those days, women wore corsets. Aunt Martha used the word stay, which supposedly in her language was the same as corset. On February 6, 1866 she cut out a stay and partially made it. On March 2 she stitched the rest of her stay. On March 5 she put bones in her stay. The definition of a stay is a corset, especially one stiffened with whalebone. No underwear wardrobe would be complete without underpants or drawers, as Martha called them. Whether they were long enough to go to her ankles, I don't know for certain. How could she know that her descendants would live in an age of briefs and bikinis?

Last but not least on the list of wearing apparel were the family members' stockings or socks, an ever-present source of need not only for new replacements but also for repairing and mending. She managed to supply the demand by knitting, or raveling and reusing yarn, when she could salvage some for making cotton stockings. How she did the latter, I do not know. Friday, March 16, 1866, she footed 5 pairs of cotton stockings. This was just part of the tasks that kept her busy quite often in the evening or whenever she had a chance to "sit for a while."

There were extra articles that may have required some sewing such as pillowcases, maybe ruffled, and bed ticks to be made and filled with straw. On March 8, 1866, Lucy finished cushioning a large chair. On March 16: "Sewed corn husk mat." On April 7 and 8 Lucy finished cushion cover to settee and put cushions on settee. On May 3, 1866 Martha was repairing back parlor carpet. On another day Lucy made Martha a band for her hair. On January 21, 1867, Martha started a buggy cushion and the next day she finished it. On September 5, she sewed on a horse blanket and the following day she finished it.

Prior to December 16, 1865, all the sewing was done by hand. On that date Schuyler purchased a sewing machine. Two days after the purchase, Mr. Olmstead came to teach them how to use the machine. From that date forward the word stitched began to appear in Martha's notes, indicating that some of the slow and painstaking handwork had been eliminated. The first evidence that she was using her new convenience was early in January, when she stitched tucks for Lucy and stitched drawer bottoms and facings. On January 16 she stitched ruffles on pillowcases. On June 19 Mrs. Barnard called in the morning. Martha stitched a little for her, the beginning of occasional stitching for others outside the family. In some cases she may have been paid for using the machine on articles for friends or neighbors, since at that time a sewing machine was not part of every household's equipment. Thanks to 16 year old Schuyler, his gift was somewhat of a luxury, probably a showing of appreciation for all his homemade clothes and providing an easier way to continue to do so on pants, vests, waists and coats, even an overcoat, all made after the arrival of the sewing machine.

No account of household activity in the 19th century would be complete without an explanation of some of the work involved in producing handmade quilts, typical of the frugal life style in the Gillett home. Discarded dresses were washed, ripped up and cut into blocks and strips for quilts. On September 24 Martha washed and ripped her bombazine skirt, worn and ready to be recycled after she had mended it several times. On February 14, she had commenced her bed quilt and that day spent most of the forenoon getting a pattern to fit. Aunt Martha sewed the blocks.

February 16: "Sewed and cut blocks. February 18, finished cutting blocks for quilt, also strips to set them together." On February 25: "Lucy was cutting blocks for her quilt. I cut strips for mine." Sewing the blocks together was an ongoing process. Finally, on September 30 Lucy put on her quilt, meaning on a frame to be quilted. A neighbor quilted some for her. On October 1 her quilt was ready to be taken off the quilting frame. On October 3, Martha was quilting with the help of Mrs. Barnard, who did so all afternoon.

Relaxing at Home

Granted, much time in the mid 1800's was used to do necessary daily chores, but there were activities that provided relaxation, enjoyment and relief from never ending tasks. In this category was the custom of calling. Friends and neighbors went back and forth to each other's homes for short visits, sometimes for a specific errand and sometimes just to talk, not able to use the telephone as we do today. Hardly a day went by with out someone coming to call, not always one person, perhaps two or more. The time of day might be morning, afternoon or evening, especially teatime, middle or late afternoon. Martha faithfully made a note of who came to call, and also, where she and Lucy, either together or alone, went to visit others. Certain names appeared repeatedly on the calling list, many of them neighbors on West Main Street as were the Barnards, Salmons, Watkins, Moshers and others.

Other happy times were when members of their family, particularly Aunt Ann's married children, came for an extended stay of one, two, or three days or longer. The Gilletts took their company for rides, often including a stop at the cemetery and, depending on the time of day, may have served them afternoon tea with biscuits, cake or some other pastry. A special evening treat might be butternuts and popcorn.

Another tasty snack was parched corn prepared for their family members or for visitors, usually in the evening. Thursday, February 2, 1865: "Mrs. Salmon and children over here. Parched corn." The Salmons lived next door on the east side. On Friday, March 23, 1866, Lucy and Aunt Ann had gone to a meeting. Martha parched corn for herself. On May 30,1866 Lucy parched corn for her friend, Caroline Watkins. On February 19, 1867 Lucy and Martha had been at the Watkins. They returned home and found the Yorks girls who "staid" for the evening. "We cracked butternuts and parched corn." Aunt Martha did not give directions for parching corn but my son-in-law's computer connection to the Internet became a reference source and produced a helpful explanation. The pioneers had eaten parched corn, often as trail food, most likely by the Gillett ancestors, when they were migrating from Connecticut. First the corn on the cob had to be dried by suspending it in a hanging position. In the early days, dry kernels were heated for less that a minute in a skillet or spider with some bacon to make the kernels swell up and turn brown, while being constantly stirred to prevent burning. The light to medium color indicated the parching was finished. This method could be modified by smearing a thin layer of grease or none at all in the cooking pan. Anyone wanting to make parched corn today can follow the same directions. It is important to remember to barely cover the bottom of the skillet with dried kernels and to keep a cover on the pan during heating time. Modernized preparation can be in a microwave oven in about five minutes at medium-low heat. Through the years, regardless of how people have made and eaten parched corn, it has started out as a dry, crunchy morsel that has become sweeter as the eater has chewed, with a flavor like nothing else. If the Gilletts used their cook room stove to heat their corn, imagine the tempting aroma that reached the guest seated in the front parlor. The custom of serving nuts with parched corn continues today, like the Gilletts' butternuts, because the oil and moisture of the nuts combine delightfully with the flavors and dryness of the corn.

Going Downtown

Diary entries about going downtown and buying certain items indicate that Lima merchants and industries supplied shoppers' needs in a wide range of merchandise. Some of the purchases recorded in 1865 follow. On January 3, 1865 she wrote, "Lucy and I went downtown in the evening. I bought me a bowl and pitcher." February 5, "Lib and I went downtown, paid for inhaling tube. $1.50. Father bought table spread." April 12: "Bought material for Schuyler's coat." April 24: "Bought some picture frames." May 1: "Bought piece of factory for Schuyler's pants and stair carpet." May 27: "Lining for Schuyler's pants and vest." A new dress for Aunt Ann and a sewing machine were other purchases in 1865.

Trips downtown to shop in 1866 included purchasing apples, nine coffee cups and saucers, photographs, a broom, a wash stand, picture nails; and several trips to the photograph gallery, the milliners and the hardware store.

In 1867 there were more trips to the milliner ship. Martha went to the slaughterhouse for meat. March 24: "Schuyler got a wagon at Pat Burns." April 20 Martha went downtown to get some tea. May 15: "Got spirits of ammonia for Lucy." June 1: "Had pin mended."

There must have been many other purchases not mentioned in the text, when she wrote simply "we went downtown." However, in the back of each volume is a section for itemized cash account listings, both received and paid. This does not include food expenditures or a complete listing of other purchases or receipts but gives an idea of the many reasons for going downtown. Sewing supplies were in constant demand, as shown by the following items: spools of thread, cotton .10; silk .05, each; buttons, 2doz. .35; 2 papers of pins .20; $1/2$ yrd. Elastic tape .05; dress braid .10; thimble .06; Sewing machine needle .08; whalebone .15; skeins of yarn one of cotton .15, one of wool .22; one yard of muslin; 12 yrds of seeded delain $5.40; 10 $1/2$ yards of alpaca; shoes $2.00; bosom pin $2.50; gloves $2.40; pin mended .15; photographs $1.50; bonnet frame .50; postage stamps 2 for .06, 3 for .05, 8 for .24, 6 for .18.

Going downtown included a stop at the Post Office to receive mail or sometimes to send letters or buy stamps. The first Post Office in Lima was in the first store, Tryon & Adams, east of the village. It was later moved to 9 Rochester Street and still later to the Gordon block, where it remained for 60 years, until the block was torn down in 1936. It is believed that the diary entries about the Post Office refer to the Rochester Street location, which was within walking distance from the Gillett home on West Main Street. Once in a while they rode downtown, but usually they walked to the stores and the Post Office.

Following is a partial listing of merchants, etc. in business in Lima in the year 1873, according to the survey made by F. W. Beers. Since there were many changes in ownership in the early and middle 1800's, it is difficult to pinpoint exactly where the Gilletts shopped. In spite of the dealers' name changes, the availability of needed items shows that Lima was definitely a self-sufficient community.

General Merchandise:
> Chambers & Watkins: Dealers in Dry Goods, Hats, Caps, Boots & Shoes, Carpets, Wall Paper, Groceries, etc.; East Main Street.
> Mitchell, W. D.: Dealer in Dry Goods, Hats & Caps, Groceries, etc.; 16 Ellis Block, Rochester Street.
> Stevens, A. L.: Dealer in Groceries, Provisions, Crockery, Stone Ware, Wood and Willow Ware, Yankee Notions.
> Gilbert, H. and O. S.: Dealer in Groceries, Provisions, Crockery, Boots & Shoes, Flour & Feed and agent for Averillis Chemical Paint.

Hardware:
> Hannah & Hawley: Dealers in General Hardware, Stoves & Tin ware, Pocket and Table Cutlery, Guns, Pistols, Merchandise and Builder's Material of every description.

Manufacturer:

    Dartt Brothers: Manufacturers of Carriages, Wagons, Sleighs. All kinds of repairing done at short notice.

Tailors:

    Foreman, J.: Merchant and Taylor, Dealers in Ready Made Clothing, Cloths, Cassimeers, Vestings, & Gents Furnishings & Agent for the original Howe Sewing Machine Improved; East Main Street.

    Hurd, S. & Co.: Merchant Tailors & Dealer in Ready Made Clothing, Clothes and Trimmings and agent for Singer Sewing Machine.

The Burying Ground

With the organization of the first M. E. Church on West Main Street came the need for a cemetery for departed members. In the year 1828, a location on College Street, near the Seminary but on the south side of the street, was chosen for a graveyard. The Gilletts made their first trip to the cemetery for the year 1865 on March 4th for the burial of Frankie. Four other family members had preceded her in the cemetery: a baby brother in 1845, another brother George in 1860, sisters Mary and Amanda and mother Martha in 1863.

Spring brought not only a change in the weather but also added work for the Gilletts and others who maintained their family plots. In 1865 frequent trips to the burying ground (as Aunt Martha referred to it) began the 20th of March and continued on a regular basis through spring, summer and part of the fall. The visits continued through the years 1866 and 1867 on a schedule similar to that in 1865, with slight variations in starting times. Often, Martha and Lucy went together. Sometimes Schuyler went with them or Martha went alone. At times she wrote simply I or we went to the burying ground and gave no stated reason. Other days, she wrote they worked at the burying ground with the length of visit varying from no specified time, to two or three hours and, once in a while, all day.

The season began with carrying soil, sowing seeds and planting roots. As the season progressed, the family was kept busy with shearing the grass, weeding and watering. Several kinds of flowers: violets, verbenas, phlox, lilies, geraniums, etc., made the family plot a garden of color enhanced by hanging baskets and bouquets of fresh flowers which they carried from home, especially during the summer and early fall.

In 1865 they went to the burying ground 39 times between March 20 and October 22, in 1866 76 times between March 3 and November 3 and in 1867 52 times between April 13 and November 23. Whenever the Geneva relatives came to visit the Gillett family, their stay included trips to the cemetery.

All the time Martha, Lucy and Schuyler spent working in the cemetery was not burdensome, but rather a labor of love. There were times when they went simply to feel closeness, a sense of comfort and to remember. On July 3, 1866 she wrote: "At 8 P.M. I am seated by Libbie's grave. One year ago today we laid her here." On August 15: "Here with my book resting on my Mother's headstone I write, about 7 P.M." In July of the same year she had written: "Here at the close of day am I seated by the graves of loved ones, a precious place." This one quotation speaks for itself, a revelation of the motivation for faithful caring of their loved ones' resting place.

Sundays

Sunday was like no other day of the week. Aside from writing about preparing breakfast and doing the necessary chamber work, rarely did Martha mention activities other than going to church, usually twice, to morning and evening services. There were exceptions, when she stayed home all day. This happened when she was not feeling well or when the weather was not favorable. However, on Sunday, February 6, 1866, a cold winter day, she and Schuyler went to morning service. Father and Martha went to evening service, where they had a fire in one stove and all attendees sat huddled around it. Because she was a member of the M. E. Church, she attended morning services there in its Rochester Street location, where Mr. Kellogg was the pastor in 1865. Martha often made a note of his choice of scripture. On January 15, he finished his last lecture in a series of evening sermons on the rules of the M. E. Church.

Israel Herrick Kellogg was born in Rutland County Vermont, August 2, 1812. In that year, his family moved to LeRoy, N.Y., where he attended schools, until he went to Genesee Weslyan Seminary. He joined the Genesee Conference in 1833 and, as a faithful worker, continued as a pastor for many years. He served in Lima for two terms from 1864 to 1865. He was followed by A. Sutherland from 1865 to 1867 and by William Benham from 1867 to 1870. The Gilletts attended services conducted by all three pastors during their respective years in Lima.

Attending Presbyterian churches did not prepare me to interpret the following diary entries: Sunday, April 22, 1866. "Went to love feast and remained until after communion." Sunday, April 21, 1867. "Father and Lucy went to love feast and to the other services." Seeking the advice of Free Methodist friends, I learned that a love feast was a special service observed by those present to deepen their feelings for one another as members of one family united by love. After the distribution of bread the people circulated among themselves to take from each other pieces of bread and to speak to one another with words of appreciation and affection. During the sharing time, the people might stand to form a circle, clasp hands and sing "Blest Be the Tie That Binds". The tradition of breaking bread together dates from the early Christian community, was practiced by the Moravians and later became a service of the Methodist Episcopal and Free Methodist Churches. Beside sharing of bread, the exact parts of the service might vary from leader participation, to include singing, testimonies and prayers by the congregation. Consequently, it is difficult to identify the particular order of service in the Lima M.E. church. Because Martha wrote about the communion service following the love feast, it is appropriate to note that Holy Communion, by the use of elements that are consecrated, is dedicated to worship of God. One way to explain the difference between Holy Communion and the love feast is to refer to Jesus commandments as found in Matthew 22: 37 and John 13: 34. "Love the Lord your God with all your heart, with all your soul, and with all your mind." and "Love one another as I have loved you."

Evening services were prayer meetings. Once a month the members of three churches gathered for a union service in one of the three churches: M. E., Baptist, or Presbyterian. On Sunday, March 19, 1865, the College President Dr. Lindsay gave his first sermon in the M. E. Church and returned to do so again on April 2. On Sunday, May 21 Martha wrote: "Very warm showers in the afternoon. I went to church in the morning and to College Hall in the afternoon. Prof. Draper preached. Went to prayer meeting in the evening." This was one of the Sundays when she went to church three times, something she did occasionally, as was the case again on June 15, when she went to morning service and to hear Dr. Lindsay preach at 3 P.M. in the M. E. Church and Dr. Anderson at 7:30 P.M., a good illustration of cooperation between the church and the college. Another example of sharing leadership between the church and the college was on Sunday, July 9, when she went to a union temperance meeting at the Baptist Church. Henry Draper and Prof. Steele addressed the audience.

So what did Aunt Martha do on the Sundays when she was home all day or most of the day? To be sure she did not sew, or bake or clean. Meal preparation was simple. The second meal after breakfast was lunch, rarely dinner, with no mention of having afternoon tea. It is obvious that reading was permissible. On September 24, 1865, she was reading the life of H. H. Rogers. On October 23, she finished reading the New Testament. On June 14,

1866 she read in her repository and read in the Bible. January 23: "Read in different books and took a nap." February 24: "Read the 'Rural' through and several chapters in the Bible." On Sundays there was a break in the daily calling. If someone called, it was to accompany Martha to church.

Sunday, March 5, 1865, was a day Martha would never forget for two reasons. It was the day after the funeral of Frankie, her 18-year-old sister. In the writer's own words, "a long day" but she did go to church in the evening. There she met Rev. Kellogg's older daughter, Frankie, whose 18th birthday was on the same day as Frankie Gillett's burial. That these two, Martha Gillett and Frankie Kellogg, should meet in the midst of Martha's sorrow was a blessing that proved to be the beginning of a lasting and enjoyable friendship. At first, the two became better acquainted during customary calling, when they saw each other at their homes. During the middle of May, when there were indications that Libbie was not well, Frankie called on the Gilletts on May 13th and again on May 20th. Four days later in appreciation for Frankie's friendship, Martha took her a bouquet of flowers. On the following day, Frankie was with her father when he came to baptize Libbie. On the fatal day, when Libbie passed away, Dr. Barnard, Addie Yorks and Frankie were there to give comfort and support. After the funeral, Frankie was not home for a while, but Mrs. Kellogg continued to call on the Gilletts. On July 19 Frankie returned home and the very next day was at the Gilletts' home. On July 29 Martha called on the Kelloggs and took Frankie riding. Relieved of the care of her dying sister and still grieving over her passing, Frankie's companionship became relaxation and therapy for Martha. During the month of August, Martha recorded at least three times when the two went riding: to the springs on the 8th, to Smithtown on the 23rd and a third time with no destination mentioned. On the 26th they went to the cemetery together. During the month of September, the calling back and forth continued, including Frankie's coming to the Gilletts for tea. On Sunday the 17th they were at church services together. Then on September 18 she wrote: "Frankie Kellogg called for the last time." The thought came to this writer, "Oh no, is she going to die also?" My suspense was relieved, when I read the next day's entry: "Mr. Kellogg's people left for Geneva," meaning he was leaving Lima to serve in the Geneva Methodist Church. Martha did not see the Kelloggs again until her trip to Geneva from November 17 to December 1, 1865, when she had a happy reunion and several visits with Frankie and her family before her return to Lima. In the year 1866, she did not go to Geneva, but she and Frankie kept in touch by letter. Of the 48 letters that Martha wrote that year, almost half of them (23) were to Frankie, who answered about an equal number of times. During 1867, Martha visited Geneva again, between October 10th and November 5th. After several chances to be with Frankie and her family she wrote: "Frankie Kellogg called on me for last time." Martha returned to Lima about 7 P.M. that day.

Special Days

Having learned that Sunday brought a change in the weekly routine, one wonders what the Gilletts did on special days that came once a year such as the Fourth of July, Thanksgiving and Christmas. The journalist's own words tell whether there was any kind of celebration or recreation appropriate for the occasion:

July 4, 1865: Pleasant day. Did very large washing. Many of the Lima people gone to Rochester to celebrate the Fourth of July. I went to the burying ground after tea. Caroline Yorks called.

July 4, 1866: Rainy in the forepart of the day. Picked strawberries, worked butter and did a variety of jobs. Carried a bouquet to the cemetery. Lucy at Watkins both afternoon and evening. The Moshers had fireworks. (The Moshers were neighbors with property adjoining the Barnards on West Main Street toward the west.)

July 4, 1867: A warm day in the afternoon two very hard thunderstorms. Cows and horses killed by lightning. At ten A.M. an oration delivered in College Hall. Students had a picnic. In the evening, Mrs. Barnard invited us over there to see Annie's fireworks. She had large crackers and small ones, large and small torpedoes.

Dr. Barnard's granddaughter's noise makers give us some idea about what was available for family use in the middle of the 19th century, aside from public demonstrations, the community tolling of bells, firing of cannons and guns, all reminders of the first Independence Day observed in 1776, long before Congress declared July 4th a legal public holiday.

The history of Thanksgiving in this country began with the first celebrated by the Plymouth colonists during the second winter in the New World. The custom spread from Plymouth to other New England colonies. On November 26, 1789 President Washington issued a general proclamation for a day of thanks. For many years there was no regular Thanksgiving Day in the U.S. In 1830, New York had an official Thanksgiving Day, and other northern states soon followed its example. In 1863, President Lincoln issued a proclamation setting aside the last Thursday of November in the year as a day of Thanksgiving and praise to our beneficent Father. Two years later, in 1865 Martha was in Geneva visiting her relatives on Thursday, November 30. She stated that her cousin, Libbie Salvage, with her daughter and grand children came from Seneca Falls to be with her sister and family. Although Martha did not identify the gathering as a Thanksgiving Day celebration, probably it was, especially since she was a guest there too. On Thursday, November 29, 1866 she wrote: "Thanksgiving. Prof. Steele preached at Presbyterian Church. Lucy at C. Watkins. I hemmed under skirt. We had oysters for dinner, a special treat, as was having a crack of butternuts in the evening." Thursday, November 28, 1867: "I went to a church service. Mr. Benham preached a grand good address. Lucy and I were at Dusinberres for dinner. Met another guest there, Mr. Wright. Went to meeting in the evening."

In the year 1865, the day before Christmas was Sunday: "Warmer. Some snow in the morning. I and my sister rode in the cutter to and from church. Christmas Eve there was a union prayer meeting at the Baptist Church. I did not attend." On Monday, Christmas Day, she and Lucy looked over drawers and boxes and worked most all day at it. In the evening at the M. E. Church, there was a diary on the Christmas tree for Martha from Schuyler. She gave him a Bible, a cap and a diary. On the day before Christmas in 1866 they washed and hung the clothes outside. Lucy did general housework. In the evening she and her sister went downtown. Eunice called. On Christmas Day, Martha picked and dressed two chickens and did other work. Lucy and Martha went to the Baptist Christmas tree. Had a jolly good time. Mrs. Sutherland received a sewing machine. On December 24, 1867: "Lucy and I were at Dusinberres quilting. Shumway was sick. She made me a present of the quilt. Lucy and I went to the Presbyterian tree. Father brought us a pair of felt rubbers." December 25, 1867: "A warm and pleasant day. I spent most of the day at Dusinberre's quilting. Took it off about 9 P.M. Lucy with me. Mr. And Mrs. D. at Mr. Swartz for dinner."

As a contrast to the merry making and partying on the New Years eve in today's culture, the Gilletts' behavior on that day and evening reflected the way they approached the coming of the new year. Sunday, Dec. 31, 1865 Martha went to church in the morning and heard Prof. Bennet preach. This was no different from every other Sunday in the year. On the other hand, Father and Schuyler did something they could not do at any other time during the year. They went to the New Year's Eve watch night service at their church. Although we have no record of the watch night service at the Lima M.E. church, the accepted conception of the occasion is that with others they were encouraged to evaluate the past year's responses to exhortations to live righteously, to be thankful for the providence of God and to make new commitments to their God, whose faithfulness they trusted for the future. This special year end service might start as early as a 6 P.M. and continue to midnight, while sermons were interspersed with singing, prayer, Scripture readings and personal testimonies, all part of their worshipful conduct.

December 31, 1866, Martha's notes show that it was a typical Monday with washing, baking and calling on the neighbors. In the evening they enjoyed eating ice cream and went to bed at eleven o'clock.

New Year's Day 1865, She wrote that they went to church in the morning and evening with no reference to other activities.

New Year's Day 1866, a Monday, they did their usual housework. Martha and Lucy went to the store and bought nine cups and saucers. Schuyler attended a student sociable.

New Year's Day 1867, they did some baking and the usual housework. Again, they had homemade ice cream, the only indication they did something special. They went to the meeting in the evening and invited their friend Caroline Watkins to go with them. It may be true that some families enjoyed gatherings for meals considered sumptuous in the mid nineteenth century, but according to all that is known, the Gillett family did not participate in celebration gatherings on the first day of the New Year.

More Comings and Goings

In spite of the many time consuming tasks necessary for keeping house, there were times when family members went riding in one of their horse drawn vehicles, either sleighing or wheeling depending on the condition of the roads. According to Aunt Martha the family owned a cutter and a buggy. At one point Schuyler washed the carriage. A buggy was classified as a type of carriage. So it is not certain that the Gilletts had two separate vehicles in addition to the sleigh. Whether the reason for leaving the house was for relaxation and pleasure or necessary errands or a combination of both, Martha wrote about who went where and when. The village of Honeoye Falls appeared often as a riding destination for a number of reasons, one being to see the family physician, Dr. Gibson. Usually when medical treatment was the cause of the trip, it provided a chance to call on Uncle Asa and Aunt Lucy (He was

John Gillett's brother.) Quite often the visit included having tea with their relatives. At other times, they went to Honeoye Falls solely to see Dr. Gibson or to call on the other Gilletts, maybe even to have dinner with them. In the year 1865 they made at least 15 trips to Honeoye Falls, most of them starting in January and continuing through June before the deaths of Frankie and Libbie. At times, Father might go alone after medicine or for some other reason. On February 18: "Lucy and self went to see Dr. Gibson." May 30th: "Lucy, Lib and I went to Honeoye [Falls]." June 23rd: "I took Aunt Ann to see Dr. Gibson." There were many times when she wrote simply she and another person went riding, especially with Frankie, before she died and many times with Libbie before her death. On June 20, 1865, shortly before Libbie's passing away, she and Libbie rode to the college, sat in the carriage and heard the speeches delivered on the steps.

Although a railroad did not come to Lima until the 1890s, the town was by no means an isolated community in the 1860s and had not been since the early 1800s. "Upon completion of the State Road in 1809 from Albany to Buffalo, the stagecoach line was used extensively for travel across the state, the fare being 6 cents per mile and 14 pounds of luggage allowed for each passenger." It was fortunate for the Gillett family, especially Aunt Ann, that the route between Lima and Geneva was traveled daily by the stage. In 1820 Ann had married William Alcock. The couple had 11 children, all born in Geneva between the years 1821 and 1840. Ann's husband, William died in 1855. After John Gillett became a widower, he married Ann, his sister in law, in 1864 and she came to live with the family in Lima. At that time six of her grown children were still living and she made frequent trips on the stage to visit them in Geneva, all of whom were there, except Elizabeth married to George Salvage and living in Seneca Falls. Martha wrote about her cousins coming to visit the Gilletts. Ann's son William came on the night stage on August 29, 1865. On August 31 Aunt Ann and William started for Geneva. On October 24, another son Charles came on the stage to visit.

In November 1865, Martha had a well-deserved break from her busy days taking care of her family in Lima. On October 16 she and Schuyler left for Geneva and arrived at 11 A.M. They began their stay at Ann and George Hemiup's. Ann was Martha's first cousin. That afternoon she went to George Alcocks (another first cousin). The next day her dear friend Frankie Kellogg called on her. Also, she and her cousin Martha went to the cemetery and down to the lake. The next day, Sunday, she and Martha went to the Episcopal service and to the M. E. in the evening. On Monday she spent the day at George Alcock's where she saw Martha at tea time and Ann in the evening. On Wednesday, November 22, a little after 10 A.M., she took the railroad cars for Seneca Falls at 11 A.M. and arrived at Salvages a little after noon. The next day Schuyler went back to Geneva. On Friday, she and her cousin Libbie went down the street and walked around town. On Saturday, she went back to Geneva on the 2 o'clock train. On Sunday, November 26, she went to Trinity Church in the morning and in the evening to the M. E. with Frankie, whose father was pastor there. The next day she and cousin Martha went to the bank, then to mile point. Tuesday she went to Charles Alcock's for dinner. Also she and Ann went to William Alcock's for tea and spent the evening there where she saw her cousins and Frankie again. On December 1 she and her cousin Martha went on the boat after dinner, then she left the Hemiup's about 3 o'clock and arrived home in Lima in the evening. On Saturday she was back to the old routine: baking, picking up things and trying to "regulate" and doing a vast amount of talking. She had spent two weeks away from home, had talked, dined and had tea with her cousins, enjoyed walks, had gone to church in both Geneva and Seneca Falls, had been on a boat ride, had ridden in the stage and in a railroad car. Surely the family enjoyed hearing all about her visit, especially Aunt Ann, who listened to news about her grown children.

In the year 1866, she recorded more about coming and going on the stage and otherwise. On February 4, Charles Staley and family came in the evening stage. They stayed until Friday, when they left in the 9 o'clock express. Saturday was the M. E. Sabbath School picnic at Conesus Lake. Thursday, June 14: "Father, Lucy and I went to Rochester. Left home about 5 A.M., returned a little after 7 P.M." For this trip, I assume, they went by horse and buggy. Saturday, September 29: "Henry left in the morning stage for Nunda." Friday, October 5: "Mrs. Chamberlain came in the Rochester Express." Tuesday, October 9: "Father and Schuyler started for Chautauqua."

Especially in the year 1867, according to Martha's notes, there is evidence that an alternative to taking the stage was going by rail from Honeoye Falls to Geneva. On February 26, she wrote: "Father took visitors from Geneva to the Honeoye Falls depot." On October 10, 1867, she wrote "Schuyler brought me to Honeoye Falls Depot. Left there, arrived in Geneva at 11 A.M." Her visit in Geneva was similar to the one in 1865. She spent time at Kellogg's and was with Frankie to go downtown and to church. Again she went to Seneca Falls. She and her cousin Martha went shopping, got Lucy a dress and returned to Geneva in the four o'clock train.

Father's Business

Considering the Gilletts' apparent comfortable life-style for their time, one wonders about their financial support. How Father John earned the money that provided for their needs and some luxuries typical of nineteenth century living. The data supplied by census records for 1855 and 1865 show that he was a butcher. Added to this information are Martha's references to other activities that supplied income. These varied somewhat during the years she kept a journal. In 1865 on Jan. 7th, she wrote that Father and Schuyler went to the mill and on Jan. 13th Father drew his logs to the mill. The next day he drew corn stalks. Beginning Jan. 14th he made seven daily trips to the mill between that date and April 21st. There is nothing to indicate the type of mill, or its location except that, on Jan. 21st their trip to the mill included a stop at Uncle Asa's for dinner. This would lead one to believe the mill was in or near Honeoye, where Father's brother and his wife Lucy lived. Also, to be able to draw logs and cornstalks, he owned a team of horses and a wagon. To add to the uncertainties listed above is the fact that on Dec. 9th, Father sold out his business, but Aunt Martha did not state what it was.

In 1866 he was definitely involved in butchering. On Jan. 3rd he went to Avon with hides. On Feb. 20th he killed his beef and on April 2 he began to butcher sheep. With the arrival of spring and warmer weather, the butchering business came to a halt and Father turned his attention to farm related work. In May, Father and Schuyler ploughed the Gillett lot and sowed oats there to provide feed for his livestock, particularly his horses. They had to put the colt in Parker's pasture and the cow in Chamber's lot, indicating their own property did not provide enough grazing land for their animals. In the fall, Father resumed his butchering connected business by making several trips after cattle, including one to York and two to Avon, followed by killing beef Oct. 29th, pork Nov. 2nd and on Dec. 12th Father and others killed 10 hogs, when they took advantage of cooler weather.

Charles Dusinberre and Martha

On Mar. 29, 1867, in Martha's journal a new name appeared, that of Charles Dusinbery not accompanied with any explanation of how the Gilletts happened to know him well enough to invite him to their home as follows: "Thursday March 29, 1867 Charles Dusinbery came here to tea and staid all night." He had been moving his father's goods from Honeoye Falls. Two days later: Charles Dusinberre here to breakfast and dinner. One thing is certain; the fact that during the brief time Martha had been with Charles, she learned how to spell his name, changing it from Dusinbery to Dusinberre. On April 1st Charles' father took possession of Ms. Clark's place. From that date forward Lucy and

Martha began calling on the Dusinberres. The first visit was on April 10th and on the following evening Aunt Ann and Father went to welcome the new residents to their home in Lima on Genesee St. (Ms. Clark's place appears in this location on the Lima page in the *Gilletts' Map of Livingston County New York* from actual surveys under the direction of J.H. French of Syracuse New York. John Gillett 517,519 & 521 Miner Street, Publisher, 1858, Philadelphia. During the months of April and May the Gilletts and the Dusinberres, especially Martha and Lucy, were getting to know each other through calling. In June Martha's notes describe other activities that indicate a growing friendship. On Sunday June 9th Martha went to evening meeting with Mrs. Dusinberre and on June 10th Martha carried some of Dr. Barnard's asparagus to Mrs. Dusinberre and on June 27 Lucy gave Mrs. Dusinberre flowers for a bouquet. In the meantime on June 22nd the name Shumway appeared in the diary. (All I know about her is that she lived with the Dusinberres.) On that day Martha and Shumway took a ride as far as Sterling's. The frequent calling continued during the summer months. Again Shumway and Martha were together riding, when they had Dusinberre's horse. They went to the cemetery, called on Mrs. Sutherland and had a pleasant time. On Tues. Sept. 24th Martha went to Dusinberre's to see their new stove. A few days later, there was another new development, a foretelling of more to come. "C.D. came home with me after prayer meeting." Early in October, Martha and Lucy finished their quilts. On Sat. Oct. 5th she went to the cemetery after her geranium tree and gave it to Mrs. Dusinberre. As has been recorded in this account, Oct. 10th, 1867, was the beginning of her trip to Geneva. As I wrote previously, she had a pleasant time with relatives and the Kelloggs, especially Frankie. While she was visiting, there were two significant notations, which made me wonder. On Friday Oct. 25th she began to embroider drawer bottoms and on Oct. 29th her cousin Mary gave her pieces for patchwork, the latter to be used for making another quilt. Even more significant was her arrival in

Honeoye Falls on Tuesday, Nov. 5th. Charles Dusinberre came to the cars for her and they arrived home about 7 P.M. After washing and ironing and regulating at home, Martha found time to be at Dusinberres on Nov. 8th and 9th.

On Sunday Nov. 10th she went to the evening service where Carlton Wilber preached. She had the pleasure of Charles Dusinberre going home with her. This was the first time she used the word pleasure to describe being with Charles. On Sat. Nov. 16th, Charles took Martha to an event at the college. This was another new development, Charles actually taking her to an event, unlike previous times, when he just took her home afterwards. She wrote, "I went accompanied by Charles D. He was with me till midnight", another first. On Nov. 19th Shumway and Charles spent the evening at Gilletts. The next day she was at Dusinberres a little while. On Thursday, Nov. 21st Martha wrote, "Charles spent the evening here. I made a contract with him." Again, her words were not embellished with emotional expressions, not even in the privacy of her diary. In reality this was a promise that a marriage at some future date would ensure that they would spend the rest of their lives together. In other words they were engaged.

Barnard-Gillett Connection

How did it happen that the names Barnard and Gillett appeared together, first in the history of Rome, N.Y., in the early 1800's and continued to be closely associated through the rest of the century in Lima, N.Y? A review of Rev. Barnard's story brings to mind the fact that the pastorate of Rev. Moses Gillett was in the Rome church, supported by John Barnard Sr. and it was there, under Rev. Gillett's guidance that John junior decided to begin his training for the ministry. "The church in Rome was then congregational and he was licensed to preach by the Oneida Association, in September 1816 at Verona. He preached his first sermon in Rome, and for nearly two years thereafter made his home with his father who was in ill health and needed his assistance."[54] At the same time he was constantly engaged in missionary work as an itinerant minister, preaching the Gospel in different settlements of the region, including Utica and Whitesborough.

Rev. Barnard went to Lima, August 1, 1818 by invitation of the Congregational church, and preached for five Sabbaths. At the time, he was under partial obligation to preach in Waterloo, which he subsequently did and decided in favor of settling there and so informed the Lima church. Learning soon afterward that a friend of his, licensed with him, desired to go to Waterloo, he acted by reversing his decision and accepting the call to Lima. There he continued to live, after his installation in the Lima church on Feb. 3, 1819. Beginning with the completion of the cobblestone in 1836, he and his family lived in Lima on West Main street, directly across the road from the Gilletts, until his death in 1872.

Was it a coincidence that the Gilletts and John Barnard became acquainted as neighbors in Lima or had they known each other before? The New York State census records for Seneca County in 1810 and 1820 show that the Gilletts lived in the township of Romulus in 1810 and in Junius in 1820, only a few miles from Waterloo. It is tempting to guess that the Gilletts may have met John Barnard, when he was an itinerant minister in their area. If this were true, on the occasion of their meeting Rev. Barnard could have asked if they were related to Moses Gillett, who had been his mentor and friend in Rome, N.Y. Their response could have depended on how much they knew about their ancestors. It is likely they thought they might be related to Moses but did not know how. This same question had been on the mind of this writer, until she learned from extended research that Moses and Alexander Gillett were actually cousins, several times removed.

If this writing were a work of fiction, the story would reveal that the Gilletts had met and heard John Barnard preach and were so impressed with his personality and message that, when the opportunity presented itself, two of their sons decided to buy land directly across the street from the acreage owned by John Barnard in Lima, N.Y. Truthfully, it is not so easy to answer the question, but proof of their closeness as neighbors is in the deeds to their properties, the maps of Lima for 1852 and 1858 and Aunt Martha's diary. Her writings included the relationships between the Gilletts and the Barnards for three years in the 1860s, but the families had been neighbors since the 1830s. The Barnard's three sons were born when they were in Lima but not on West Main Street. The Gillett family increased with the addition of seven children, after they settled in Lima. The Barnard's first son died as an infant and the Gilletts first son died at the age of twenty-nine in 1845. Nevertheless, the Barnards were able to sympathize with the Gilletts at this point in their lives.

The many diary references to the members of the Barnard family show that the Gilletts and the Barnards saw each other often in their homes. On Monday, Jan. 23, 1865 Martha wrote: "Not pleasant, washed, and baked a cake for surprise. Attended surprise party at the Barnards. Had a good time." Living in the cobblestone were Rev. Barnard, age 75; his wife, Ann, also 75; his sister, Abby, 76; his widowed daughter-in-law, Lucina, 47 and his granddaughter, Annie, 12. There is no indication about the honored guest at this happy occasion.

Not long afterwards, the Gilletts needed the support of caring neighbors, because 18-year-old Frankie was not well. Abby Barnard's name appeared among the callers. By Feb. 17th, Frankie's condition had worsened to the point that she was confined to her bed, where she needed to be watched either by a family member or a good friend. During this critical time, before her death, Abby, Mrs. Barnard and Rev. Barnard came to call. Then on March 1st, when Frankie died, among the friends present were Rev. Barnard and his sister Abby. Frankie was laid out by Mrs. Arnold and Mrs. Barnard. During the month of March, after Frankie passed away, there was more calling back and forth. Lucina and Annie came often. One day Annie was at Gilletts four times.

The month of April brought a change in the calling pattern, when Lucina called twice and brought Libbie oranges. On April 25th she was there several times and on April 28th she brought Lib some asparagus. Some time went by before Lib and Martha went to see Dr. Gibson, and on that same day Mrs. Barnard brought Lib some fish. Two days later she brought Lib asparagus and Miss Abby called. This special display of attention to Libbie showed that all was not well with her. However, on May 17th she was able to call on the Barnards, probably to thank them for their kindness to her. During the month of June, Martha and Libbie went riding frequently, sometimes more than once a day. On June 21st Martha went to Mrs. Barnard's to can strawberries, another act of gratefulness for the good neighbors thoughtfulness. On June 25th, the day of Libbie's baptism by Mr. Kellogg, there were five callers, Rev. Barnard, Miss Clark, Delia Yorks, Lucina and Mrs. Arnold. The next day, ten concerned friends came including Lucina. On June 28th six people came three of them Barnards, Mrs. Barnard, Lucina and Abby. One of the visitors brought Lib a bouquet. Libbie's life came to an end on July 1st. Among those present were Rev. and Mrs. Barnard. He talked and prayed. After Libbie died, between 11 and 12 o'clock, at the age of 26, Mrs. Barnard and Mrs. Winams laid her out. Like they were during Frankie's illness and death, the Barnards had been an ever-present source of support and comfort. Surely, Martha expressed her thankfulness for their loving care, when she visited the Barnards three days after the funeral and on July 12th when she took them a bowl of yellow berries. On Wednesday, July 26th, Martha was not feeling well (no wonder) and Mrs. Barnard came to the Gilletts several times to lend a helping hand.

Since Martha and Lucy were skilled in the art of sewing, they were able to help others who were less talented or not blessed with a sewing machine. This was the case with Lucina and Mrs. Barnard, when they needed assistance. Lucy made a ruffle for Lucina and helped her cut out a sacque, (a loose gown). Martha stitched a braid on a dress for Mrs. Barnard and did other stitching for her at various times. On Dec. 12, 1866, Lucy was at the Barnards sewing for Lucina afternoon and evening. Maybe she was making something for Annie for Christmas.

When they entertained in the evening, they needed extra light. On Dec. 18th, 1866, Lucina went to the Gilletts to borrow a lamp, because the Barnards were having a surprise party. On May 22, 1867, to prepare for having a church social, Martha went to the Barnards to borrow a lamp. On July 27th, Lucina did lots of work for Martha, when she was not feeling well. Without a doubt, the two neighboring families made a difference in each other's lives that showed respect and thoughtfulness on a day-to-day basis.

There is no recorded evidence that members of the Gillett family attended special Presbyterian events, other than funerals, or that Dr. Barnard tried aggressively to attract them to his church, in spite of the fact that the families were close neighbors and friends. One exception was on Aug. 7th, 1867, when Lucy went to a Presbyterian Society meeting with Mrs. Barnard, who took her to and from there. The Gilletts remained loyal to the M.E. Church, although they went regularly about once a month to union prayer meetings, when the Methodist Episcopal, Baptist and Presbyterian Churches took turns hosting the gatherings, evidence that an ecumenical spirit did exist.

Toward the end of 1867 and the final pages of the diary, the subject of quilting received attention. Probably Martha knew that her marriage might be sometime soon. On Oct. 3rd she wrote: "Pleasant day. Lucy baking. I did a variety of things. Quilting on my quilt. Mrs. Barnard quilted all afternoon and was with the Gilletts for tea." "Oct, 5th at Dr. Barnard's twice." "Wednesday, Nov. 13th I was at Dusinberres. Came home and found Mrs. Barnard here." This was the last time the name Barnard appeared in Martha's diary.

Following Martha's final journal entry in December 1867, the next years brought many changes. Charles age 40 and Martha age 35 were married in 1868. Whether they moved to East Avon, before Lucy's death in 1869, or after, there is proof they were living in East Avon on July 27, 1870, according to the New York state census, which states that Charles was a farmer, age 42, that his wife Martha was keeping house and they had a one year old daughter Mary. The 1875 census shows that they still lived in East Avon, with the added information that Charles was a farmer and sawyer and that his brother-in-law Schuyler Gillett was living with them. Furthermore, in a *History of Livingston County*, published in 1881, there is a brief reference that Charles Dusinberre was the proprietor of the steam and cider mills located one-half miles east of East Avon.

In the meantime, there had been other changes in the Gillett family household after Lucy had died at the age of 32 in 1869. The 1870 census for Lima lists Schuyler as a laborer, but there is no trace of his father or stepmother, indicating they were not with Schuyler, but I do not know where they were. There is no indication that they went to live with Charles and Martha. The 1872 survey map of Lima shows new owners across the street from the Barnards. They are Mrs. Beckwith, Mrs. Beadle, S. Coventry, F.S. Stevens and J. Chambers, with no sign of the Gillett name. The next known information is that John Gillett died in 1875 and his second wife Ann returned to Geneva, where she and her first husband William Alcock had raised their children. She died there Oct.7th, 1884, age 79 years.

**Abby Barnard
John Barnard's sister**

Meanwhile, the years between 1868-75 had brought many changes within the walls of the cobblestone. Not long after Martha's notation about Mrs. Barnard visiting the Gilletts on November 13th, 1867 Mrs. Barnard died in 1868, actually before the death of Lucy Gillett in 1869. Once again, sympathy for bereavement had characterized the connection between the two families. Just two years after Charles and Martha had been living in East Avon, Dr. Barnard died on Sunday morning, Mar. 24th, 1872. Although they were no longer living in the house across the street, the Gilletts who were able to offer their sympathy were Martha, Schuyler, John and Ann. The surviving Barnard family consisted of Abby, Lucina and Annie.

Death of John Barnard

With the death of Dr. Barnard on Sunday, Mar. 24th, 1872, the time had come to celebrate his life, an opportunity to say, that his life was the best sermon he ever preached. The funeral took place Wednesday, the 27th. "The church was appropriately draped in mourning, and crowded above and below, with a congregation that largely represented all the neighboring towns. About a dozen ministers were in attendance."[55] Rev. Levi Parsons read appropriate passages of Scripture and Rev. A. L. Benton offered prayer. "Rev. Henry Kendall D.D. then gave an address in which he very happily and discriminately exhibited the characteristic excellence of the deceased, whom all concur in regarding as the Model Gospel Minister."[56] Following spoke John B. Richardson, who was his neighbor, while settled in Pittsford for many years and assisted him in a revival in 1836. "In conclusion, a Presbyterian of some twenty-five years standing gave a sketch of his life and closed by expressing congratulations to the family, church and community that it was their privilege so long to witness the radiance of such a burning and shining light, and enjoy its hallowed influence. Then we bore the precious remains to their last resting place in the rear of the sanctuary and interred them beside those who had gone before, and as we did so, there was not a man in all that saddened group but felt assured that our venerable and beloved brother, who had always been a faultless specimen of the perfect Christian gentleman."[57]

The eyewitness account quoted above was written by Rev. Joseph Page, then pastor at East Avon. Gleaning more information about his life, his preaching of the Gospel and his service in the larger church is possible by studying two church histories, one from an Historical Sketch prepared and read by the author, Elder W. R. McNair on the occasion of the 100th anniversary of the Lima Presbyterian church, October 1st, 1895. A quote from the title page is as follows: "Oh where are kings and empires now? Of old that went and came, But Lord thy church is praying yet. A thousand years the same." The other historical pamphlet is Two Hundred Years of Presbyterian Life in the Lima Community 1795-1995, taken from "Two Hundred Seconds" read to the congregation during the bicentennial and based on the church history in process of publication by Frances S. Gotcsik. Another resource document is a biographical piece by Rev. Joseph Page whose writings are quoted in the preceding paragraph. His further remarks about Dr. Barnard include characteristics of this remarkable man, his kind fraternal spirit, and his love of peace, his Gospel labors and long life as a perennial fountain of blessed influences, not only to the community but also, to all the region round about. "His gentle loving spirit led his brothers associated with him to regard and speak of him as Beloved John. It equally endeared him to his people"[58]

Aunt Martha's record of the connections between the Barnards and the Gilletts give a sample of Dr. Barnard's relationship with the community. Although her writings covered events limited to a period in the 1800s, for sure, his gentle, loving spirit had given comfort and support to many who were saddened by illness and the loss of family members or friends including the Gilletts, whose three year old died in 1845 and George in 1860 at the age of twenty-nine. Mary, Amanda and Mother Martha died in 1863, Frankie and Libbie in 1865 and Lucy in 1869.

In the midst of all this, Mrs. Barnard was his companion for over fifty years, while she contributed as a pastor's wife and good neighbor. It is unfair to the relationship to dwell on the melancholic side of their lives without the assurance that rejoicing in happy times was part of their life in the cobblestone, the surprise parties, the marriage of couples, the church socials, the joy of seeing Annie grow from childhood to teenager and God's gift of peace beyond human understanding. Indeed, it had been a privilege for the Gilletts to live across the street from the Barnards, but the Gilletts reaching out to the Barnards by offering assistance and friendship showed that they truly did love their neighbors as themselves.

A New House of Worship

Following Dr. Barnard's resignation in 1856, membership in the church had continued to rise from a total of 189 to 220 during the pastorate of Rev. Robert Kellogg and to 287 during the leadership of Rev. Alphonse Benton. In 1870 Rev. Benton resigned and was replaced that year by Rev. A.H. Carliss, who guided their growing congregation through the events that led to the vision, financial support and construction of a new church building, which remains to this day at the center of the village of Lima. For some years, the church had sponsored an ice cream social on the Fourth of July on the church lawn, but in 1872 the location changed to Richard Peck's home, the large stone house at the northwest corner of East Main Rd. and Bragg Street. At this strawberry social of historical importance, the women persuaded the men to help them raise subscriptions to build a new place for worship as well as a new session house. Previously, in their homes, they had held refreshment socials to raise money for a session house. Pledges were given that day providing $12,000 of the estimated need of $25,000. The ensuing unusually cold winter made everyone willing to attend coffees and socials to provide financial support to replace the old building that could not be heated comfortably. What a change this was from an earlier time, when worshippers sat in an unheated sanctuary!

In the spring of 1873, the ladies came to the rescue by raising $1,500, the needed balance to reach the goal of $20,000 to start the work. The old church was torn down, but these frugal Puritan descendents devised ways to recycle some of the lumber. In fact, in a Lima home today is a beautifully preserved chest of drawers made from pews that stood in the old building, until it was demolished in May, 1873. After a series of delays, due to changes in structural plans and over expenditures, new subscribers contributed more pledges, making possible the project's completion. The building was dedicated on October 15, 1874, about two years and four months after that historic strawberry social in Mr. Peck's home. The legacy of these dedicated people is a structure that has been used by congregations for 130 years, still impressive and still attractive and still a centerpiece in the village of Lima.

Demolition of church

My Grandfather

I am pleased to report that the time has come to write about my grandfather, Schuyler Liddiard Gillett, who never saw his grandchildren, because he died before we were born. His birth date was January 4, 1849, making him the youngest of eight living children, all girls, except George, who was eighteen, when his baby brother joined the family. Regretfully, I do not have much information about his boyhood years, and I have to depend on the supposition that he started school in the original red brick schoolhouse and finished his elementary education in the newer building. It is likely he went to Sabbath school in the M.E. Church on Rochester Street, after it had been moved from the West Main Street location in 1843.

His descendents can be grateful that Aunt Martha mentioned Schuyler in many of her diary entries, a primary source of information about his teenage years of 16, 17, and 18. Many times, when Father went someplace, Schuyler was with him. This was true on Sunday, when the two of them went to evening meeting. The father son companionship could have been, in some ways, a learning experience for a young teenager not attending school, as when they went to the mill together, when they ploughed their lot, when they worked on the road, or when they went for cattle.

In 1865, from September 20 to 30, Schuyler worked for Mr. Walker. It is likely there had been other chances to earn money that year, because in December he was able to buy a sewing machine. One year later, at the age of seventeen, he told his sister he would be worth $20,000, when he was twenty-five years old. These ambitious thoughts must have convinced him that he needed something to help him reach his goal. Soon after making that statement, he bought himself an arithmetic.

Still totally dependent on a loving family for his room and board and his homemade clothes, in return, he shared responsibilities, by occasionally helping with the washing, working in the cemetery, washing the carriage, and shoveling snow. On

December 6, 1866, he picked a duck and a chicken. In 1867, when Father was a partner in running a store, Schuyler ground meat and helped make sausage. No doubt, there were other chores, not mentioned by Martha, that gave him opportunities to be helpful, such as milking the cow and feeding the chickens.

There were times that Schuyler harnessed the horse for riding in the buggy, when he was the driver to take his sisters downtown, to Dr. Gibson's in Honeoye Falls, for joy rides in Michigan or some other place, to entertain company or to take them to and from the train station.

During the frequent times, when Father and Schuyler went to Rochester, the teenager may have held the reins, while the hours of togetherness fostered a time for conversation and closeness between Schuyler and his father, who had a dual role in parenting, after the death of his first wife Martha, when Schuyler was fourteen years old.

Perhaps as a gesture of fondness and trust in Schuyler's developing maturity, Father gave him a colt. Imagine his delight, when he harnessed his colt and drove him for the first time on December 17, 1866. Since it snowed most of the day, and the sleighs were out, it is possible the colt pulled the cutter. In the following new year, at the age of eighteen, Schuyler made a move that showed he was on his way toward independence and self support, starting his first business venture by buying a wagon on March 21st. Thereafter, in the same month, most likely driving his colt, he went to Honeoye station to get a load of shingles and to Avon to get another load. A little later, he drew two loads of hay, one for Mr. Gilbert, the other for someone not named. However, it cannot be said that his teenage years were times of all work and no play. It must have been fun for him to go with his sister to visit his cousins in Geneva and Seneca Falls in the fall of 1865. He enjoyed skating on Long Pond in the winter and going fishing with his friends in the summer.

After reading his sister's last writings about him in her diary, in the year 1867, we have to depend on census data to determine where he was and what he might have been doing. In 1870, he was listed as living in Lima and working as a laborer. In 1875, he was living with Charles and Martha Dusinberre in East Avon and working in the saw and cider mills managed by his brother-in-law. Aside from being related in marriage, and closely associated in the mills, another relationship developed. It was Schuyler's partnership with Charles in managing a liquor store on Rochester Street in Lima. According to trustworthy recollections, this venture did not satisfy his expectations for the future, and he abandoned it in favor of making soft drinks. Using a secret recipe for the ingredients and for the process of combining them with filtered water, he showed his ability to be inventive, resourceful and successful in his "pop" factory, located on Livingston Street, a half a block from its West Main Street intersection. The man he hired to deliver his pop could be seen on the high back seat of the horse drawn red-wheeled wagon, ready to make calls in neighboring communities. Resting on springs, an elevated green box was a custom made carrier, designed to prevent bottle breakage over rough roads. This was accomplished by fitting the crates of bottles inside so that they used the space with no room to spare. The span of his delivery destinations covered stops at East Avon and Avon on one week day, Hemlock, Livonia Center and Livonia another day, Bloomfield and Victor a third day, with other stops on succeeding days. This wagon, in a dissembled state, has been preserved to this day. Many years later, a collector found a Farnsworth Gillett pop bottle on the shore of Hemlock Lake, where the historic Halfway House used to be. In the 1880 census, Schuyler was registered as a resident in the American Hotel managed by "Lem" Farnsworth, who was his partner in the "pop" business, exhibited by an old postcard directed to Farnsworth and Gillett. It is an order for sodas requested by Mr. Outterson of Caledonia, N.Y., where it was mailed on May 2, 1881 and cancelled in Lima on the same day. Some of the old Farnsworth Gillett bottles are still available for collectors today.

By the year 1881, Schuyler was 32 years old, well on his way to becoming a confirmed bachelor, but something happened which made a difference in his life. All I can do is call attention to certain circumstances that may have contributed to this change. "Lem" Farnsworth's wife's maiden name was Frances Markham whose family lived in a cobblestone house, about three miles northwest of Lima, on what is now the Heath Markham Rd. Frances had a younger sister Minnie. At the time of the 1880 census, when the Farnsworths were living in the American Hotel, Leonard J. was 33, his wife was 26 and their son Samuel 6 and Schuyler Gillett was 31. In that year, Minnie, age 18, lived with her family on the farm. It is logical to assume that Schuyler and Minnie were introduced to each other by his business partner "Lem" and his wife, who was Minnie's sister. From what I know about Schuyler, I suspect he would not consider matrimony, until he was financially able to support a wife and family. He was on his way to meeting this requirement, as his "pop" business thrived. Far be it from me to speculate about when he popped the question, but I have a copy of a wedding invitation that reads: "Mr. And Mrs. Augustus Markham request the pleasure of your presence at the marriage of their daughter Minnie to Schuyler L. Gillett, Wednesday, May eleventh, 1887 at 5 o'clock P.M. Lima N.Y." Their marriage certificate is signed by A.F. Colburn, officiating clergyman. The groom was 38. The bride was 25.

Markham Genealogy

Who were the Markhams and how did it happen that they were living 3 miles north of Lima at the time of Schuyler's and Minnie's marriage. This seems like a good place to begin tracing the events that led to the residency of a prominent Lima family. Actually, both the Markhams and the Gilletts had ancestors that came to this country from England, although the Markhams' English roots predate those of the Gilletts. One lineage book even shows that a certain Marcam commanded a division of Saxon spearmen at the battle of Hastings (1066) and survived the battle. The Markham family of Tuxford, Nottinghamshire, was in residence and possession there since the time of Henry I, 1159. One of the direct descendents of these early forefathers was Sir Robert Markham, who lived in England in the late 1500s and early 1600's, and had a son William, born in England in 1621. Eventually, William came to America and died in Hadley, Mass. in 1690. He was the first Markham to live in this country. William's son Daniel, was born in England and immigrated to Cambridge, Mass., November 1, 1671 and died in Enfield, Conn. May 6, 1760. Daniel's son Joseph, born in Enfield December 8, 1717, died of smallpox, April 3, 1761. Joseph II born in Chatham, Conn., June 25, 1742, lived in Ackworth, N.H. and married Mehitable Spencer of Hartford, Conn. His children were Joseph and Mary. Joseph, born in Chatham, Conn., was destined to be the first Markham to migrate to New York State, after he left his father's home in Hew Hampshire in 1791, when he was 21 years old. The destination of his journey westward was Lima, which he reached by walking on Indian trails. There he assisted in raising a barn, the first frame building to be erected. He located upon land in Avon, N.Y., that same year (1791). In 1798, he married Hepsabeth Peabody, in Rochester. Living in their log cabin, their eleven children were Diana, Sarah, Willard, Spencer, Joseph, Betsy, Malintha, Laura, Guy, Augustus, and Mehitable. He cast his first vote for George Washington for President at Timothy Hosmer's log cabin in Avon. He held office as Commissioner of Highways eight years and served in other important town offices. Respected and admired by his contemporaries, Joseph Markham continued to reside on his farm in Avon until his death in 1867, age 97. His wife Hepsabeth (Peabody) Markham died at the age of 72.

The Markham family history resumes with the following biographical account of Joseph's son, Augustus, born in Avon in 1820. He received his education in the district school in that community and worked at the old homestead. He married Louisa Parmelee in 1851 and the same year he and his brother, Guy, purchased 121 acres of farm land in Lima, including a cobblestone house, but did not live in the house until the fall of 1858. His family grew with the birth of nine children: Jennie, Francis, Malintha, Charles, deceased at the age of 21, Clara H. who died in infancy, Minnie, Lottie, Joseph and Guy. While he and Louise were raising their family, Augustus acquired more farm acreage, reaching, in 1860, a total of 400 acres to accommodate his herd of sheep, one of the largest in Lima. At this time, Augustus was involved in a $17,000 distillery business with a Mr. Chamberlain. Evidence of continuing prosperity is in the 1870 census that registered the Markham real estate valued at $37,000. In that same year, the family members living in the cobblestone were Augustus 48 farmer; Louisa 37, keeping house; Jennie 17, teaching school; Frankie 16, at home; Malintha 14, attending school; Charles 12, also in school; Minnie 8, in school; Lottie, in school; and Joseph at home. Changes in the 1875 census include Guy, at the age of 4, the youngest child; and Catherine Doyle 24, a domestic servant, not able to read or write. Minnie was 13 and she lived in the cobblestone 12 more years, before she became Minnie Markham Gillett.

The marriage of Schuyler and Minnie united two separate lines of the descendents that had developed from English roots. Ancestors of both families immigrated to America first to Massachusetts and later to Connecticut, where the Markham descendents lived in Enfield and Chatham. The Gillett predecessors were in Windsor, Simsbury, and Suffield, before some of the Gilletts came to New York State in the early 1800s. Joseph Markham came to Lima in 1791. Recall that Alexander and Sarah Gillett came in the early 1800s to Seneca County and their sons, Asa and John, settled in Lima in 1833. Finally, the year 1887 brought the merger of the two separate lineages, when Schuyler Gillett and Minnie Markham were married.

Schuyler and Minnie

During the first years of married life, they had two children, Erson, born August 6, 1888 and Alfred born December 12, 1890, exactly where in Lima I do not know. I vaguely remember my Grandmother Minnie saying her children were born in a house on Livingston Street. This would seem logical, since my Grandfather's pop factory was located on that street.

According to a *Directory of Livingston County*, published in 1894, Schuyler was listed as manager of the Bailey Engine Company, that made rotary engines, and he was listed as a bottler on Livingston Street. He continued to be a bottler, still washing all the bottles by hand, until he invented and patented a shotting machine that mechanically added small pellets and a cleansing solution to the bottles and agitated them to complete the cleaning process.

Markham house

In the meantime, while Schuyler's business ventures were being successful, Augustus Markham was having farming troubles. A number of reasons had contributed to his misfortune, including advancing age, failing health and lack of help from his two sons who did not have the interest or necessary skills to manage a 435 acre farm or to be their father's successors. In 1896, after several months of being confined to the house, Augustus died from what was diagnosed as stomach cancer. His obituary stated he was one of the most prominent citizens of Lima. He was a Democrat and one of the most influential men in his party and had held various town offices, including supervisor and excise commissioner. In the same year as Augustus' death, his son-in-law, Schuyler, bought the farm to save it from foreclosure. For sure, this move helped to relieve the anxiety of his wife and other family members, who were Mrs. Jennie Dennis and Mrs. Frances Farnsworth, both of Rochester and Mrs. Malintha Watkins, Mrs. Lottie Quinn, Joseph and Guy of Lima.

The Lima Bottling Works continued to provide income to support the many changes that followed with the dawn of the twentieth century. In the 1900 census, when Erson was 12 and Alfred was 10, their parents were renting the cobblestone, previously owned by the Barnards and others. Schuyler had spent twenty-one years of his youth living across the street from this house.

In 1902, Schuyler and Minnie made the decision to purchase the cobblestone, which, in 1879, the Barnards had sold to new owners Joseph and Sarah Chambers. The Chambers sold the property to William and Phebe Huyck in 1890. According to the deed, made the first day of August one thousand nine hundred and three, Schuyler and Minnie Gillett bought the cobblestone on West Main Street in Lima New York from the Huycks. A number of reasons must have convinced them that it was a wise move to buy the house they had been renting since 1900. Apparently, they had become attached to their rented home. In addition, Schuyler was financially able to invest in a permanent residence and the seven adjoining acres and last but not least, Minnie had lived in the Markham cobblestone for twenty-five years of her young life and no doubt, was delighted with the prospect of raising her family in a similar abode.

When the Gilletts bought the Barnard house it had been remodeled by buyers who had owned the residence during the early and late 1800's., the Chambers and the Huycks respectively Exactly who had made the changes is unknown, but the following description, written by Frances Gotcsik, adequately describes the nineteenth century additions:

> the sweeping Queen Anne style veranda with a profusion of finely crafted woodwork, including a spindle frieze, segmented arches with pendants and sunburst motif in corner panels between support posts, a projecting cross gable over the main entrance with checkerboard motif, and an elegant balustrade with diagonal and diamond-patterned railings. The original Federal period front door has been replaced with Queen Anne Style double-doors, but the entrance retains its fluted pilasters, corner blocks, and three-part transom typical of the early nineteenth century. Thus, the Barnard house evolved from a rural farm dwelling on the fringes of the early village, and by the late nineteenth century, became a fashionable gentleman's residence near the heart of the bustling village.[59]

Shortly after the Gilletts became owners of their stone house, Schuyler began to make more changes. An addition to the back of the house provided space for a new kitchen, pantry, and dining room on the first floor; and an attic, walk-in closet, hallway and bedroom on the second floor. This added another bedroom to the original four in the upstairs, which Schuyler remodeled to include a bathroom and hallway at the head of the stairs in the cobblestone structure.

The entrance to the kitchen was from the wrap-around porch. A door on the south side of the kitchen opened into a small hall that gave access to a stairway to the attic on the second floor. Also, from this hall one could go through another door to a back porch and down to ground level on steps at the west end of the porch. Schuyler's final touch to the addition was installing a slate roof over the new part and the original cobblestone. True to his ingenuity for inventing, he made a cutter to score and cut the desired shape of the shingles.

Another major improvement, beside the addition to the house, was building a barn with a main floor for road wagons and buggies, a loft for hay storage, and a basement for a stable with two stalls. Also, on the lower level was a one story enclosure with stalls for cows. Other farm buildings included a cow barn and a chicken coop. Having a need for metal parts in connection with his pop business and the Bailey Engine Company, Schuyler built a workshop, where he could apply his mechanical skills. In a small building across the alley from the barn on the east side, he installed a natural gas driven stationary motor to operate various metal working machines, via a series of belts and pulleys.

Architectural details of porch (side entrance)

Queen Anne double doors and pilasters

Addition built by Schuyler Gillett

With the handicap of not knowing the exact sequence of Schuyler's accomplishments, it is difficult to identify the timing of another interesting development. Somehow he discovered existence of a natural gas reserve deep within a part of his seven acres. Geologists admit they do not know the precise origin of this natural resource but with the help of chemists, they have theories that explain what happened through the ages. A very brief description attributes the source to billions of tiny plants and animals that lived, died and deteriorated to a sediment that eventually became buried under layers of rock. Subsequently, "under heat and pressure, the organic sediment decayed, forming gas and oil. The gas and oil escaped through deposits made of limestone, sandstone and other porous rock. Hard layers of rock above these deposits have kept the gas and oil from leaking out. The gas in the earth is usually sealed under great pressure, so that when it is tapped, it comes roaring to the surface with hundreds of pounds of pressure behind it."[60] To take advantage of this natural resource on his property, Schuyler hired someone to drill a well that made possible the release of the gas to be piped into the basement of the cobblestone, through the stone foundation, with walls the thickness of one and a half feet.

This account of his endeavor omits many of the steps that were necessary to produce results, however; my cousin Erwin tells about an incident that happened when his father, Alfred, was a curious, adventuresome boy. His father had dug a ditch to accommodate the pipe that led to the gas well. In spite of warnings to stay away from the ditch, Alfred's curiosity got the best of him. He went into the ditch, lit a match and was blown out. His injury from the explosion was minor compared to what his father inflicted, as a punishment for his son's disobedience. As a strict disciplinarian, Schuyler did believe that sparing the rod would spoil the child.

Augustus Markham portrait

Leading from the well to the cellar was a pipe that had a reducing valve necessary to lower the pressure of the gas from the well, making it usable for household and other purposes. By a system of pipes and valves to the kitchen and elsewhere in the house, the gas supplied power for the cook stove and lights. Also, a pipe to the workshop provided gas to operate the engine that ran the machinery there. Still later, the attachment of a generator to the gas powered engine produced electricity for use in the house, making it the first in Lima to have the advantage of this convenience. According to family members, this statement is true, but I have no actual data to support the inferred claim about the other houses in Lima.

Erson and Mabel

The early 20th century brought not only building and property changes, but also the maturing years of Schuyler and Minnie's sons, who were approaching middle and late teens. This was especially noticeable in Erson, the older one, who had become friendly with a certain young lady, who lived with her family on the first farm east of the Lima reservoir. It was known as the Vary farm. Her parents were George and Jennie Bartholomew and she had a sister Jennie and a brother Walter. Many years later, Jennie, who became my aunt, told me what happened on the evening of November 15, 1905. There was a birthday party at the Bartholomews to celebrate Mabel's becoming 15 years old. Some of the invited guests were young people from Lima, including Louise Gillan (Green), Mabel Hamilton (Hosley), Bessie Briggs, Gus Sharpe and Alfred and Erson Gillett. Mabel's mother, who became my grandmother, told Mabel's younger sister Jennie, age 13, she could stay up for the party, if she would take a teaspoon of kerosene for a very bad sore throat. Under protest, she took it with sugar on the spoon. Then she was present, when Erson gave Mabel a ring that was a combination of red stones and pearls in a gold setting.

Who were the Bartholomews and how did it happen they were living in Lima about one and one half miles from the Gilletts on West Main Street? In April of the year 1900, the family had moved from Ossian, New York to the Markham farm and were living in what had been the Markham cobblestone. Father George had been hired by the owner, Schuyler Gillett, to oversee business on the farm that continued to be their home for the next three years. George Bartholomew came to work for Schuyler Gillett, owner of the house and property since 1896, when Augustus Markham was threatened with foreclosure. According to the 1900 census, George, born in September 1850, was 49 years old. His wife Jennie, born in May 1858, was 42. Their daughters, Mabel 9 and Jennie 7, were born in November 1890 and February 1893, respectively. Their five year old son Walter was born in September 1894.

During their stay on the Markham farm, all of the children attended the district's one room schoolhouse on the northwest corner of Dalton Rd. and the Heath Markham Rd. Aunt Jennie told a story about something that happened, while she was going to the Dalton Rd. school, within walking distance from her home. On a certain day during recess, some of the kids decided to follow the tracks on the Honeoye Falls trolley line. It was 2 o'clock before the hikers returned to school. As a punishment for their late arrival, the tardy pupils were dismissed for the day. Because it was too early to go home, Jennie found a hiding place, until four o'clock, when she returned home at the usual time. She said her Mother never knew about the exploring venture.

The Bartholomews had about three years to enjoy getting nicely settled and adjusted to their life on the Markham farm before another move. This time they went to the place where Mabel had her 15th birthday party in 1905. The reason for the change of residence was likely connected with the sale of the Markham farm to Edward F. Dibble for use with a seed company. Apparently, George Bartholmew's expertise as a farm worker was not needed in the seed company. In 1904 he had been hired to work on the Vary farm, where the family lived for three more years.

I do not know where the children went to school during that time or whether Erson and Mabel attended the same school. Obviously, before and after Erson gave Mabel the ring, they had chances to see each other, perhaps beginning when Mabel lived on the Markham farm. It has been noted that Erson's father was Mabel's father's employer. When the Bartholomews moved to the Vary farm, Erson and Mabel had the advantage of living closer to each other.

While the Bartholomews were still living on the Vary farm, the year 1906 brought changes within the Gillett household. In the Gillett cobblestone, under the care of her daughter Minnie, Olive Louise Markham died at the age of 73 years, after a long illness. Her obituary stated she had lived in Lima most of the time since her marriage to Augustus in 1851. Mr. and Mrs. Markham's hospitality was known far and near, as no one ever went hungry from their home. She had been Augustus' widow for ten years.

One year after Louise Markham's death, George Bartholomew was hired by Mr. Dibble to return to the Dibble farm and to the cobblestone, where the Markhams had lived for nearly fifty years and where George had worked for the three years during 1900-1904. The connection between the Gilletts and the Bartholomews grew closer during the years that Erson and Alfred and Mabel and Jennie attended Genesee Wesleyan Seminary, which offered the only high school education available in Lima at that time, because the first graduating class from Lima High was not until 1919. Their social lives centered around the student societies. In addition Erson and Mabel saw each other often, while she was living with her parents and siblings on the Dibble farm. We have snapshots taken during their courtship there. Aunt Jennie said Mabel had a beautiful new gray coat, which she tore, while she was going over a fence. Erson took the coat to be mended and Mabel's mother never knew what happened.

It seems almost incredible that another move was destined to separate the two lovers, whose friendship had evolved into a romantic attachment. This time, in 1910, after Mabel received her eighth grade diploma from Genesee Weslyan Seminary, the Bartholomews moved to a farm near Geneseo. Two years later, the following news item appeared in the Lima Recorder. "A quiet home wedding occurred in Geneseo on Wednesday afternoon (April 10, 1912) in the home of Mr. and Mrs. George Bartholomew, when their daughter Mabel was united in marriage with Mr. Erson M. Gillett, one of Lima's popular young men. Rev. L.L. Swarthout performed the ceremony, using the ring service. Alfred A. Gillett, brother of the groom and Miss Jennie Bartholomew, sister of the bride, stood up with the happy couple, who, after a short wedding tour will reside in Lima."

One family story was told about the meal following the ceremony. Minnie Gillett, the bride's mother-in-law, had made rosettes (delicate pastries made by dipping an iron in batter and frying in deep fat) to serve over creamed chicken. The help in the kitchen made the mistake of putting the rosettes under the chicken mixture instead of on the top. The result was the disappearance of the rosettes on the guests' plates, much to the disappointment of Erson's mother.

Alfred's Farm

One year after Erson and Mabel were married, his brother Alfred and his father Schuyler bought a 78 acre farm east of the village of Lima. This was not a surprising move for Alfred, who had shown an interest in farming for some time. In fact, he had a herd of cattle that had grazed on a part of the Gilletts' seven acres on West Main Street. He had milked his cows in the stalls that were located in the basement of the big barn and used a separate smaller cow barn as a needed shelter for his animals. (The foundation of that building remains to this day.) Using gallon pails to hold the milk, he delivered to customers in the village. They transferred the milk to their own containers for household use, especially making butter.

In 1913, Alfred drove his 18 cattle on the highway to their new location, the farm on East Main Rd. The farm purchase included a house previously owned by Henry J. Raymond who became founder of the New York Times. At this time in his life, Alfred a bachelor, needed a housekeeper. Mabel, his sister-in-law, agreed to assume the role and she and Erson moved into Alfred's newly acquired home, where their bedroom was the front parlor of the homestead. This arrangement continued for about three years, until Alfred married Clara Hall.

In addition to giving Alfred financial support, his father had decided to suspend his pop business for a year to help on the farm, especially with building maintenance. On Wednesday, October 4, 1916, Schuyler had climbed a ladder to paint a silo. A heart attack made him fall to the ground and he died instantly. The first report to Minnie in the house was that her husband was very sick, but soon she knew the truth, that he had actually died, confirmed by the coroner, after Schuyler had been carried into the house.

Schuyler's obituary stated that he was once a student at Genesee Wesleyan Seminary and a member of the Lyceum Society. Years before, his sister Martha had written that he paid his initiation dues to the Society, but she never did write that he attended school at the Seminary. So far, I do not know when he did that, which remains an unknown without further research. A tribute in his obituary was that he was a machinist and inventor of a bottle washer and that he started the Lima Bottling Works, 25 years ago. Limited space in the Lima Recorder did not allow room for an account of his many accomplishments, but fortunately, I have been able to add a sequel, which reveals much about this ambitious, remarkable and respected man, who died at the age of 69. He was the last survivor of the Gillett parents that came to Lima in 1833. Martha, author of the diary, died in 1911. Schuyler's funeral was in the cobblestone on West Main Street. Dr. MacCormack officiated.

Children in the Cobblestone

Schuyler's death left Minnie a widow living in the big house. Lonesome and overcome by grief, she urged Erson and Mabel to make their home with her. This they did. Mabel was expecting her first child. The baby was born February 28, 1917, four months after the death of Mabel's father-in-law. She and Erson named their baby Ernest Schuyler Gillette. He weighed only four pounds and his survival largely depended on the expertise of the attending practical nurse, Mary Webb, who put him in the oven in a shoe box. This custom predated the use of hospital incubators. Two years later, Erson and Mabel had their second child, born May 3, 1919, whose birth certificate bore the name Margaret Gillette. She did not have a middle name, until she was baptized on June 13, 1920 by Dr. MacCormack, who convinced my mother to name me after him and my name became Margaret MacCormack Gillette.

Horse block in side yard with author and brother Schuyler

This seems like a good place to insert some information about Dr. MacCormack's position in the Lima Presbyterian Church, where on December 13, 1909, the congregation had voted to call Rev. William C. MacCormack as pastor, at a salary of $1,000 per year, four weeks vacation and the use of the parsonage. In succeeding years, financial problems plagued the church to such an extent that, in 1919, the presbytery recommended a house to house canvass for raising money and to use the funds to raise the pastor's salary. By 1920, membership was 106 and the current budget was $2,050. On July 30, 1920, Dr. MacCormack's resignation was accepted, because he was suffering from failing health. A copy of the 125th anniversary service shows his participation on Friday evening, when he delivered an historical sketch of the Lima Presbyterian Church. On Sunday October 3, 1920, in the morning service, an announcement formally acknowledged that Rev. William C. MacCormack had been made Pastor Emeritus of the church. His successor was Rev. Albert Anthony, who was the minister from November 21, 1921 until July 1922. Rev. Samuel Palmer succeeded him in the same month and continued as pastor for seven years.

Speaking Repertoire

It was during either the pastorate of Rev. Anthony or Rev. Palmer that Margaret Gillette made her debut in the Lima Presbyterian Church at a traditional Children's Day celebration, in the month of June, when the young children spoke pieces. Since I do not remember the occasion, I am guessing it was a Sunday in June 1922, when the pulpit area was decorated beautifully with bouquets of garden flowers, donated by church members. No doubt, my Mother had made my dress of some dainty material, maybe organdy or dotted Swiss, and in my patent leather shoes, my feet mounted the steps necessary to reach the pulpit area. With a voice that could be heard throughout the church, I recited my piece: "A bumble bee backed up to me and pushed." Many years later, Howard Allen, a dear friend of my father and the rest of the family, told me I had caused a response of laughter on that day in June 1922.

Depending on others for information about our years from infancy to the point of remembering ourselves is followed by a transition period, when a few impressive events can be recalled clearly. In my case, the next memory was within that category. Without being able to pinpoint the exact time, probably during the year 1923, I had told my Mother I wanted a baby sister. On the evening of November 1, 1924, my brother and I were called into our parents' bedroom to see a surprise. Having heard her first cry, Schuyler had some thoughts about the noise but did not guess that he had a baby sister. I shall never forget the thrill of seeing her (in her clothes basket bed) for the first time, when she opened her big blue eyes. I was one happy 5 year old and to this day have been thankful that Doris Lynch, nee Gillette, is my sister. Let this tribute serve as an introduction to what happened next.

The brief start of my speaking repertoire was followed by a much longer recitation, which I do remember. This time, some of the ladies of the church, my mother included, took part in a dramatization, which they produced on the stage of the Lima Town Hall. As a part of the performance, I was asked to speak a piece. I was either five or six. The ladies' costumes were old fashioned dresses and mine was one worn by Mrs. Taylor's son, Dean, when little boys were clad in dresses. It was red, flecked with white and gathered at the waist. The copied poem is all or part of what I spoke. My lines may have been a modified version. However, I definitely remember holding up my Grandmother's long black stocking at the end of the piece. Also, my baby sister had been born, making her the one mentioned in the poem. The show, to raise money for the church, was so successful in Lima, the ladies decided to do a repeat performance in Caledonia. I remember, when I stood in front of the women seated on the stage, there were some kids sitting in the front row of the audience and they laughed at me.

Here is the piece I spoke.

Hang up the baby's stocking
Be sure you don't forget!
The dear little dimpled darling,

She never saw Christmas yet!
But I've told her all about it,
And she opened her big blue eyes;
And I'm sure she understood it
She looked so funny and wise.
Dear, what a tiny stocking!
It doesn't take much to hold
Such little pink toes as baby's
Away from the frost and cold
But then, for the baby's Christmas,
It will never do at all.
Why, Santa wouldn't be looking
For anything half so small.
I know what I will do for the baby.
I've thought of the very best plan.
I'll borrow a stocking of Grandma's,
The longest that ever I can
And you'll hang it by mine, dear mother,
Right here in the corner so!
And leave a letter for Santa,
And fasten it to the toe.
Write this in the baby's stocking,
That hangs in the corner here.
You never have seen her, Santa,
For she only came this year
But she's just the blessed'st baby.
And now before you go,
Just cram her stocking with goodies,
From the top clean down to the toe.

By Emily Huntington Miller

And at the end of the piece, I held up my grandmother's long black stocking.

The Children's Day programs continued each year, and I always spoke a piece, but I do not remember what I recited.

Sometimes, the themes for the programs were flowers and other natural creations. Some of the children would be dressed in crepe paper costumes. One year, Esther Lloyd spoke Joyce Kilmer's poem "Trees". That made such an impression that I still remember her recitation and the poem is one of my favorites.

The Christmas season was a special time at church. When I was about eight years old, Mrs. Samuel Palmer, the minister's wife asked me to recite a piece as part of an evening service. The only line I remember is "The oaken rafters holly bedite". Spending a lot of time trying to find the poem did not produce results, so today, I am unable to quote more than what I think was the first line.

Sunday School

Thankfully, I have fond memories of Sunday School in the Lima Presbyterian Church. In the primary department, the teacher used colored pictures, about 18" by 12", to illustrate Bible scenes. My earliest memory of learning a Bible verse was "Let the little children come unto me and forbid them not for of such is the kingdom of heaven" (Matthew 19:14). The picture was Jesus sitting with little children, one or two on his lap, and the rest seated on the ground around him. This verse has stayed with me through the years and its meaning has grown with me. The simple faith of little ones is a quality that retains its significance at any age for dependence on Jesus as a Friend and Savior.

Our classes were in the fellowship hall behind the sanctuary, basically the same as it is today. Before meeting with our particular age groups, we had opening exercises, when someone played the piano to accompany singing. Everyone looked forward to having a birthday, when the one celebrating dropped pennies in a little basket, the number corresponding with the age of the child. All the children sang "Hear the pennies dropping. Listen while they fall. Everyone for Jesus. He will get them all."[61] We learned other songs that became favorites, so much so it is easy to recall some of the words. "Jesus wants me for a sunbeam, to shine for Him each day. In ev'ry way try to please Him, at home, at school, at play." And the chorus, "A sunbeam, a sunbeam. Jesus wants me for a sunbeam. I'll be a sunbeam for Him."[62] Another song that comes to mind is "Brighten the Corner Where You Are" and of course, the classic favorite "Jesus Loves Me".

The children were expected to go to Vacation Bible School during one week in the summer. Bible stories and memory work were part of the program. At an early age, I learned the 23rd Psalm. Some kind of handwork kept little fingers busy. A typical activity was making paper mats by weaving narrow strips of colored paper through slits in a square of construction paper about 6" by 8". There were other things to do. One that I recall was making objects with modeling clay.

I am unable to recall many of the details of attending Sunday School in the years immediately following being in the primary department except to say I was present and continued to learn more about Jesus.

An outgrowth of our class at church was what we called the Sunshine Club, a gathering of friends who met at each others' homes to enjoy being together. Out of the conversation among ourselves came the idea that we might do something to help someone less fortunate than we were. My suggestion was that we buy some linen toweling, sold by the yard, cut it into the length of individual towels and, by hand, do the necessary sewing to hem the raw edges of each towel. When we had completed the project, a couple of us delivered our gift to a black family that had lived in Lima and moved to a house near East Avon. At our young ages, this thoughtful consideration of the needs of others was commendable. Since I am the sole survivor who can tell about our activities in that group, there is no one to help me with adding more details about what we did.

Much more vivid in my memory is being in Mrs. Kittredge's Sunday School class, when I was in junior and senior high school. She was a religious Bible student, able to teach and guide us with our lessons and their application to our lives. Extending our togetherness were the monthly social gatherings in her home. Part of our regular routine was reciting the words of the 121st Psalm

> I will lift up mine eyes unto the hills, from whence cometh my help.
> My help cometh from the Lord, who made heaven and earth.
> He will not suffer thy foot to be moved; He that keepeth thee will not slumber.
> Behold, He that keepeth Israel shall neither slumber nor sleep.
> The Lord is thy keeper; The Lord is thy shade upon thy right hand.
> The sun shall not smite thee by day, nor the moon by night.
> The Lord shall preserve thee from all evil; He shall preserve thy soul.
> The Lord shall preserve thy going out and thy coming in from this time forth and for ever more.

and singing our theme song, "I Would Be True". Howard A. Walter wrote the words and Joseph Y. Peek composed the music.

> I would be true, for there are those who trust me,
> I would be pure, for there are those who care,
> I would be strong, for there is much to suffer,
> I would be brave, for there is much to dare
> I would be brave, for there is much to dare
>
> I would be friend of all, the foe, the friendless
> I would be giving and forget the gift;
> I would be humble, for I know my weakness,
> I would look up and laugh and love and lift,
> I would look up and laugh and love and lift.

Mrs. Kittredge always served us a nice lunch, including her good homemade rolls. In the years following her loving, faithful teaching, I have been truly grateful for my membership in her "True Blue Class" and for Mrs. Kittredge's influence on my life.

Christmas Memories

Some of the earliest recollections of my life in the cobblestone are of Christmas memories. Probably the very first was Christmas Eve, 1923, before our baby sister was part of the family, when my brother and I were told that Santa was coming that night. As the two of us were going upstairs to bed, and had mounted one or two steps, Santa appeared in the front hall window. All I can say is that we were ecstatic, as he waved and said "Merry Christmas". Our parents hurried us to the east parlor window, where we watched Santa leave all the way down the east lawn. It was dark with only a street light to show the way, and he fell as he was descending the slight embankment, before he reached the road. Many years later we learned that Uncle Howard Allen, our parents' dear bachelor friend, was the one who made that night unforgettable for two happy kids and, most likely, others on his route. When we found our presents under the decorated tree in the northeast corner of the parlor the next morning, proof that Santa had really come down the chimney were the ashes on the newspaper in front of the fireplace in the living room.

Another outstanding Christmas Eve in my memory was sometime later, when Schuyler had an unfortunate experience. As was her custom, Mother had candles burning on each of the deep, low window sills in the parlor. Schuyler had been playing with a celluloid comb near one of the candles. Whether it was deliberate or accidental, the comb caught fire and gave him a severe burn on his hand. I think this was the year my brother and I found tricycles under the tree on Christmas morning. Anxious to try our trikes during the winter, we rode them in the basement, where two of the connected rooms, the first cellar and the furnace cellar, had cement floors and gave us a good place to ride. According to my memory, Dr. Kober came to dress Schuyler's hand in the cellar, where we had been riding our trikes.

Without being able to identify the actual years I received certain gifts, I'll attempt to list some of them that came from loving family members. One year, Grandma B's creativity transformed an orange crate into a doll house. The separate rooms had curtains and rugs and were furnished with miniature metal furniture. Another time Aunt Jennie and Emma Van Duser, both school teachers, brought me a beautiful doll from Cleveland. Previously, Santa had given me a doll's bed and carriage.

Some years later, I was delighted that I received roller skates. I was so anxious to use them that I went across the street, with the key, fastened them to my shoes and learned to skate, while there were patches of snow and ice on the sidewalk. As soon as spring came, Dorothy Briggs and Nancy Osborne rolled down from the hilltop on West Main, met me, and the three of us continued to the four corners, thence on the west side of Rochester Street. It was great to skate on the smooth section of slate side walk, before we reached the College Street corner. Skating shortened the time needed to get to the schoolhouse, a welcome change from having to walk the same distance four times a day. Because Mother prepared dinner for the noon meal, we walked home and back to school during the mid-day recess. Sometimes I envied the kids who took a bag lunch to eat at school. There was no cafeteria in those days.

My memory of Christmases after our very youngest years, was being with our cousins, Uncle Alfred and Aunt Clara's family. Recall that Uncle Alfred bought his farm in 1913 and he married Clara Grace Hall in 1917. Their first child was Vernon A., born Dec. 24, 1917. Their second child was Erwin, born March 21, 1921, followed by Thelma Rosamond on Jan. 12, 1923; Emily Jean, Nov. 16, 1926 and Alfred Carmen, May 21, 1930.

Because farm chores came first, we opened our gifts in the evening. Since the families took turns, the tree (a white pine from Hemlock Lake property) and the presents were in our parlor every other year. Christmas dinner was in the dining room, in the middle of the day, when relatives gathered to enjoy a special meal, the main course often being rosettes on top of a serving of creamed chicken. A favorite dessert was homemade ice cream. Mother made the custard and my father was in charge of the freezing process by using a hand operated freezer, consisting of a bucket to hold the snow and salt and the can of custard to be stirred by a dasher turned by an attached crank. When the freezing process had been completed, a special treat for us kids was licking the ladle, in other words, eating the ice cream that remained on the dasher, after Daddy had pulled it out of the freezer can. The next step was packing the bucket with more snow, to keep the contents of the can frozen until dessert time. To enjoy this holiday meal, all of the adults sat a table extended by putting extra leaves in the middle. The children sat at a separate table. When it was our turn to have the family gathering, after dinner, Uncle Alfred's clan went home to do chores and came back for the evening's activities. In the meantime, Schuyler, Doris and I amused ourselves by shaking and inspecting our wrapped presents and guessing what might be inside.

Another delay kept us in suspense about our unopened Christmas gifts. The wait was prolonged, because all of us kids took part in a program, that included speaking pieces, doing skits, singing or playing the piano. Grandma Gillette had been our coach at practice sessions days before. With sighs of relief, after all that was over, we took turns, one at a time, opening our presents. Our Christmas Days were unique in some ways, but they were happy times not only for the children but also for the adults, grandmothers, aunts and uncles, brothers and sisters, and cousins enjoying being together.

Visiting The Farm

Christmas was not the only time we saw our cousins and their parents. Our two families visited back and forth regularly. One time our Mother and Father were taking us home from the farm in our old Cole touring car. It was summertime, because the detachable side curtains were not in place. My brother and I were riding in the two separate seats that had been raised from the floor in the space between the front and back seats. All of a sudden, I looked for Schuyler beside me and he was not there. He had fallen out of the car. My father stopped, rescued my brother and we continued on our way, making a stop at Dr. Kober's. After checking Schuyler for any broken bones, or other injuries, he said he had survived the accident in good shape.

When we were not old enough to know better, one day after school, my brother and I walked to the farm with our cousins, without getting permission from Mother to do so. We loved to go to the farm. Mother found out where we were and we had to walk home to West Main Street. Our punishment was an early supper of shredded wheat and promptly thereafter we were sent to bed.

There were many other times, when we had chances to be with our cousins and to do things that we could not do at home. Life on the farm was so different from ours in the village that we were delighted to have a chance to visit there. One of my earliest memories of being at the farm was when Uncle Alfred invited us to watch shearing of the sheep. As time went on, we often had the privilege of being present at milking time, which gave us a glimpse of an activity that was just one phase of my Uncle's dairy business. We watched the cows enter the dairy barn, one by one from the barnyard and go to their stalls. The amazing sight was seeing that Daisy, Strawberry, Fillpail and all the others had been trained to go to their stalls and to put their heads through the open stanchions, metal bars that were closed around the cows necks to keep them in place during feeding and milking time. In their separate stations, each animal had a feeding trough and drinking cup. Their food might consist of hay from the loft and/or silage, chopped up stalks of corn that had been stored in the silo. Our cousins had asked us to taste the ensilage, when they showed us the storage area, but I refused the offer. Hand milking was done by Uncle Alfred and my cousins, when they were old enough to do so. Seated on a stool beside the right side of the cow, the milker made a stream of milk flow from the cow's udder into a pail positioned directly below. Often a thirsty barn cat came for a taste of fresh milk, which the milker supplied by aiming a stream directly into the cat's mouth. To pass the time, while our cousins were helping with the milking chore, we played a guessing game. When we first started to play, only Uncle Alfred and Vernon knew the secret. Vernon would leave to a spot, where he could not hear the rest of us choosing an object. Upon his return, his father kept naming objects, until he guessed the one we had chosen. After playing the game many times, I finally figured out what Vernon and his father knew about guessing the chosen object. I had to make a promise that I would not reveal the secret of the game to anyone, however many years later my husband and I played the game with a group of friends, and to be able to do this I had to tell him about the secret, which no one guessed.

Our cousins did their daily chores, which included helping with the milking before they went to school in the morning, but they had free time, when they could enjoy playing, especially when we were visiting the farm. On a summer day, they might hitch up their horse, old blind Cub, and take us for a ride in what they called the democrat wagon, usually down the lane behind the barns. Aunt Clara had packed a picnic lunch or maybe just cupcakes for us to eat, when we reached the back lot. At other times we were always welcome to sit at the table with the family and enjoy Aunt Clara's good cooking. Her banana cake was a favorite. If my mother and father happened to be there with us for an evening visit, Schuyler, Doris and I played hide and seek with

Vernon, Erwin, Thelma, Jean and Carmen. Later we might go inside and listen to Aunt Clara and Uncle Alfred playing the piano, using their talents, as a form of relaxation after a busy day on the farm.

Playtime

If I were asked to use two words to describe our childhood, I would say they were happy and carefree days. There were several conditions that made this possible. Most important was a comfortable home provided by loving parents, that set the stage for play activities, some unique and some typical of what kids did in the days before T.V. and computers. In addition, our neighborhood chums came from families that lived across the street. They were the O'Connells: Anita, Eugene (Buddy), Emilie and Mary, whose ages corresponded quite closely with those of Schuyler, Margaret and Doris. The action took place in several different locations and was determined to some extent by where we lived. For example, the wraparound porch, spacious and lengthy, was an ideal play area on rainy days or just any day. Red light green light was a game that we liked to play. Someone was chosen to be the caller. The rest lined up three or four abreast at the kitchen end of the porch. When the leader said "green light" the other players dashed forward, until the caller said "red light". This routine was repeated, with seconds between changes of pace, until someone was at the other end of the porch. There we were, just kids, totally oblivious to the fact that our play area was significant as an example of Queen Ann architecture, nor did we know that a certain wild lacy flower was named after her.

At the kitchen end of the side veranda were five steps that led from the sidewalk to the porch. Here was where we played a game we called teacher. Someone was chosen to be the leader, who concealed some small object in one hand. He stood before the children seated on the first step, extended both fists and the other players had to guess which fist held the hidden object. The first one to guess correctly had the privilege of moving to the next higher step. The game continued, until a winner reached the top step and earned the right to be the new teacher. In the days of our childhood, there was a sidewalk adjacent to the side porch and it extended, beside the kitchen to the back porch. This sidewalk was an ideal place for a game of hopscotch.

One unforgettable summer, was when we produced a play in the loft of the barn. It was "Jack and the Beanstalk". The actors and actresses were the Gillettes and the O'Connells. Other neighborhood kids paid five cents to see the performance. For a curtain, we suspended a sheet from one of the low-level cross beams. What we used for props has faded from my memory, as well the lines of the dialogue from a script which we found in a wonderful resource volume called the *Instructor*. It contained subjects and activities of interest to children, including the poem about hanging the baby's stocking. I have not been able to locate a copy of the book.

When the Gillette kids were still enjoying childhood years, the former workshop building became our playhouse. The presence of the workbench and some machinery did not interfere with imagining a floor plan, using space for rooms, especially the kitchen area, where there were shelves for dishes. How could we know that in the future our playhouse would become, with appropriate adjustments, a real home for a young family of three, father, mother and baby, the mother being one who played there in a make believe house, but that is another story that may be told sometime as a sequel to this one. The history of the little building evolved from workshop, to playhouse, to one room home, to artist's studio, to guest house.

Another play area was the west lawn. It was an ideal, level spot for a croquet game where the Gillette kids and their neighborhood chums played often. Near the west edge of the lawn were two black walnut trees. In the fall, we raked the leaves to make leaf houses, by shaping the outline of rooms, walls and partitions with rows of leaves two or three inches wide and three or four inches deep. In other words, we could design floor plans unlimited except by our imaginations or the size of the lawn. The same location became the site for a lemonade stand, patronized by a tramp, our only customer. We were thankful that a touring car full of gypsies did not stop. This business venture only lasted for a single day.

In the winter, sliding down hill was our favorite sport. Our parents warned us not to use the slope directly behind the house, because it was not safe to try to steer through the narrow passage way between the barn and the shop. Out of necessity, my brother found a route to slide from the driveway, around the west side of the barn, then to make a left turn, after clearing the back of the barn, and to continue down the slope to the open field. Depending on sliding conditions, especially if the snow were packed with a slight glaze, the ride would be fast and long, assuredly for my brother who had belly whacked on his Flexible Flyer to get a good start. My little Fleetwing never went as fast nor as far as Schuyler's sled, but I did not miss a chance to slide down hill. One day after school, I went sliding by myself. I made it safely, until I cleared the back of the barn. Then on glazed, packed snow, I lost control of my sled and slid into a chicken wire fence that scratched my eyelid and forehead. I did not want to tell my parents about my accident and I stayed in an upstairs bedroom until supper time. When they found me, I tearfully told them what had happened.

When I went to school in Miss Coykendall's room, Dorothy Briggs was one of my first grade classmates. It was not long before we became friends and spent many happy times together playing either at her house or mine. Very often, our play area in her home was in the third floor front room, that had a raised platform at one end and a low wooden seat encircling the rest of the room. At the time, I did not know the origin of this unique part of Dorothy's parents' home, located at the top of the West Main Street hill. In 1795 Major Asahel Warner built this three story, 20 room house, one of the first frame houses erected west of

Geneva. Major Warner was a member of the first lodge of the Masonic order, organized prior to 1816 in the vicinity of Lima This explains why he provided a meeting place on the third floor of his home. In the days of my childhood, the wooden dais at one end with its two pillars remained unchanged since Mr. Warner's time. Dorothy called the room "the guide hall" and I do not know why she gave it this name.

Dorothy and I continued to be good friends, and were in the same classes in school, until she dropped out of high school during her junior year, because she was having health problems.

Hemlock Lake

If someone were asked to name the natural scenic wonders of New York State, certainly the Finger Lakes would qualify to be listed with Niagara Falls, the Adirondacks, the Catskills and others. Geologists' explanation of the origin of the Finger Lakes is that glaciers retreated northward and created lakes in valleys, where rivers had flowed southward into the Susquehanna River. The huge ice sheets caused the reversal of the drainage system by leaving damming formations at the southern ends of the river valleys. This briefly explains the formation of the eleven Finger Lakes in western New York. The six largest are Cayuga, Canandaigua, Keuka, Skaneateles, Seneca and Owasco. The others are Canadice, Conesus, Hemlock, Honeoye and Otisco. Hemlock is almost seven miles long, an average six tenths of a mile wide, with greatest depth of at least ninety feet.

Space in this narrative does not allow a thorough consideration of the many fascinating facets of Hemlock Lake history, but a few high lights will follow to introduce the subject of the lake which is a part of the cherished memories of this writer. In the early 1600s, missionaries who visited the area "told of large numbers of Indians encamped around the lake, when fishing was good."[63] More information is revealed in the account of the ravages of Sullivan's army in 1779 aimed at eliminating Hemlock area's Indian inhabitants. "There the solders destroyed large quantities of beans and corn on Seneca planting grounds near the present site of the village of Hemlock."[64]

Early white settlers near the lake were men who served in Sullivan's army. "Others followed, many of whom built their first dwellings along the lakeshore."[65] Stories are told of the first settler of Springwater "traveling over the ice with all his family and possessions. Another pioneer and his family made the trip up the lake Indian style in canoes."[66]

Soon the lumbering industry flourished in the Hemlock Canadice region. "Sawmills were erected at both ends of Hemlock Lake and huge rafts of logs were floated down the lake. In the winter, as many as 200 teams of horses and oxen were used to pull lumber north on the ice."[67]

As the lumber supply diminished, Hemlock Lake's use changed from a transporting route to an attraction for people seeking a resort area, a place to provide enjoyment away from home, especially city dwellers from Rochester. According to the book, *Up and Down the Hemlock* by D. Byron Waite, published in 1883, there were at least 70 buildings along the shore, including hotels and cottages. He named the owners and briefly described the buildings. By 1900 the number of buildings had grown to 200.

Several developments had facilitated the increased use of Hemlock Lake as a popular recreation area. A plank road completed in 1850, between Rochester and Hemlock, had made horse and buggy and stage coach travel easier. In 1860, the arrival of the first steamboat, built by George Watson, provided a new source of pleasure and profit, making trips on the lake, with frequent dancing parties on its deck. Modeled after a canal boat, it proved to be unwieldy and its use as a steamboat stopped at the end of the second summer.

The use of the Watson began what might be called the beginning of the Steamboat Era, which continued with a succession of boats from 1860 through 1883, when D. Byron Waite wrote a description of each craft and the extent of their success on the lake. The successor to Mr. Watson's steamer was the Seth Green, a smaller craft, thirty-eight feet in length, compared to the seventy feet of it predecessor but more manageable than the Watson. The Seth Green is of special interest for several reasons that will become obvious as its story unfolds. Two days before the launching date, June 25, 1874, the craft had been positioned ready for its maiden voyage, beginning in front of the Lake Shore House. On the chosen day, a crowd had gathered to witness the historical event. "By eleven o'clock the balcony of the Lake Shore House, the shore of the lake, and the rustic pass-way leading to where the young 'Seth' was safely secured were pretty well packed with young and old."[68] The launching ceremonies began with music by the coronet band of Lima and presentation of a flag for the craft by fifteen year old Miss Mattie Atkinson of Lima. A short speech by a notable followed. Then came the "Star Spangled Banner" from the band, three cheers for the steamer and three more for the Coronet Band of Lima. Then "Seth," with fifty persons on board, slowly and silently left for a trip up the lake. The Seth Green operated on the lake for four more seasons but in the fall of 1878, it was pronounced unseaworthy and laid aside, to make room for its successor the next season.

I do not have exact information about the closing of the Steamboat Era. However, Mr. Waite's account continues with descriptions and launching years of four more steamboats: Corabelle, 1879; Nelly Taft, 1880; Nellie, 1881; and the Camille, 1883. He indicated that all four steamers were still in service in the year 1883.

One of the most rewarding experiences of gathering information for this narrative has been the pleasure of finding related material in the most unexpected places. For example, Byron Waite concluded his chapter about steamboats with a reference to the steamer Wave. A quote from his book leads me to speculate about my ancestors' involvement in addition to his writings.

Under the heading of Wave, the description of the boat follows: "This little clipper is smaller than any other steamer on the lake, and quite different in many respects, from any of them. It belongs, and was run last season (1882) for the first, by Farnsworth of Lima and is exclusively a family pleasure boat. It was built expressly for the lake, and will be remodeled somewhat for the coming season."[69]

You may recall that Leonard Farnsworth was my Great Uncle, listed in the 1880 census as proprietor of the American Hotel in Lima. His wife was Frances Markham Farnsworth, sister of my grandmother Minnie Markham Gillette. Also, he was my grandfather Schuyler Gillette's partner in the pop business. I have no oral or written source of knowing how many times members of my family may have been invited to enjoy a pleasure trip on Hemlock Lake, but I wonder if Schuyler and Minnie could have ridden in the Wave during their courting days, prior to their marriage in 1887. At any rate, it is certain that Leonard and Francis Farnsworth shared the luxury of their steamboat with others, years before I had the pleasure of boat rides on the lake, not in a steamboat, but in a little rowboat, propelled by an outboard motor.

Closely related to the Steamboat Era as a time for thriving lake travel, is the arrival of a railroad connection between Rochester and Hemlock in the year 1895. In 1953, Arch Merrill wrote an article for the Democrat and Chronicle. The title of his work is "Diving Suits Sound Like Good Idea on Echo Rock Visit." A quote from his article is: "Once, six passenger trains and two freight trains rolled into Hemlock daily. The first train on the Lehigh owned Rochester and Southern was greeted ceremoniously in 1895. It was a big day for Hemlock. Excursions were run from Rochester and the fare included a steamboat ride around the lake."[70] This leads to the conclusion that steamboats continued to run for years after Waite wrote his book in 1883.

An intriguing phase of Hemlock Lake history is the development of the hotel business that accommodated the increasing influx of visitors seeking relaxation and pleasure, either transients or boarders. According to Waite, the Jaques House on the west side, not far from the foot, had been a "fashionable resort for not only transients but also for permanent boarders through the summer season and for a number of years before the arrival of the Seth Green in 1874. "[71] Preceding this event, in 1872-3, "the original building had been enlarged making a structure 36 by 42, three stories high in height and a two storied wing 80 feet in length, with very pleasant rooms, long rambling piazzas, and cool shady, cheerful surroundings. Seventy five to one hundred visitors could be comfortably cared for at a time."[72]

A short distance southward, the original building of the Lake Shore House had been enlarged, in 1874, to receive more visitors and provide a large dining room and a Dancing Hall.

Just a few years later, in 1879, the St. James opened for business on the eastern side, near the foot of the lake. Pictures of the building show a three storied structure with verandas. It was described by some as the largest and most elaborate hotel on the lake, receiving 60 regular boarders beside transients. It offered the convenience of free picnic tables located on attractive public grounds.

Proceeding southward on the East Lake Road, horse and buggy travelers could reach the Half Way House, about three miles beyond the St. James. The story of the development of this location is interesting historically, because the site became a favorite spot for exploration, years later, when this writer and her companions hiked on the abandoned lake road. Construction of the original highway had begun in 1826 and was not completed until a year later. In the meantime, men worked long hours felling the trees, clearing the land and constructing bridges to establish a route suitable for travel by horse drawn vehicles. After a hard day's work, the laborers had to climb the adjacent hill to reach the places where they stayed over night. Abner Goodrich conceived the idea of building a "double log house, below the road on the point, and moved thereto for his and their accommodation."[73] In 1827,

Goodrich erected another building which was enlarged later by the next owner and became known as the Half Way House and offered the conveniences of a hotel with intermittent periods of prosperity. It coexisted on the point with the double log cabin, which was occupied by the builder's son and later by others. Historical records list the Half Way House as one of the five hotels that attracted travelers visiting Hemlock Lake. However, recorded information does not give exact dates that indicate when its business flourished and the extent of its services.

In 1878, D.P. Ager of Springwater finished building of the Port House for boarders who wished to spend a few days or weeks at practically the head of the lake. This completes the listing of the five hotels that prospered during the beginning and height of the Steamboat Era and continued to thrive as the railroad brought more pleasure seekers to Hemlock Lake.

A history of Hemlock Lake is not complete without giving additional attention to the shoreline cabins and cottages that surrounded the lake in 1883, when Waite gave an account of each one from its origin to the time of his writing, some with more details than others. He began with facts about dwellings at or near the foot on the east side and progressed southward, naming each building and its owners, including the date of construction and giving evidence that the majority of the buildings were erected in the 1870's and early 1880's. However, a few pioneers came years before that time, an example being at the site of No. 9, Union Cottage, where a pile of stones was the only remaining evidence of a log house built in 1840. The successor, built in 1879, was "one of the most lovely and delightful places of resort on the lake."[74] Its owner was John Morley from Lima.

Some distance south of the Half Way House was No. 18, Sheep Pen Point, which was given that name, because farmers from Bald Hill came annually to wash their sheep in the lake there. Years later, three bachelors were spending time in their "cozy summer home" on the point where sheep had waited for a dip in the lake years before.

Another early settler was Perez H. Curtice who "moved an unoccupied, small framed building from Hemlock Lake village on the ice in the winter of 1840-1. Here he lived alone, working occasionally a few days at a time at his trade (millwright) until 1849. In the year 1864, he disappeared and his fate was not known, until his remains were found in a fair state of decomposition in a farmer's field. His habitation Curtice Point No. 24, was torn down and portions of it were afterwards used by boys as a raft."[75]

From Waite's guide to the cottages on the eastern lake side, I have chosen one more with distinctive connections to early lake history. A building, completed in 1875 by D.B. Waite received the name of Hermitage. In the summer of the same year, "The first landing built south of the center of the lake was built here July 26"[76], where the Seth Green landed a few days afterward. All the business for the south end of the lake was done here for three consecutive seasons. "The location is remembered as the only free picnic ground on the lake"[77] up to and including the year 1883.

No. 38 on the west side near the southern end was a shelter 12 by 12, where George Atwell of Lima rested, when he was on excursions fishing for trout, This was one of several cabin-type places located on the west side.

No. 51 was McQuaid's boat house that served the needs of the Bishop, who had a country home on the hillside above the lake.

No. 58 was Echo Rock Cottage that had existed since 1881, when L.A. Pratt of Rochester had "erected an imposing home on the elevation of west Echo Rock."[78] Recall that in 1953, Arch Merrill wrote a newspaper article about this spot, noted for its inclusion in Indian legends that told of Indians hearing their voices come echoing back to them, making them believe the responses came from others of their kind, who had departed to Spirit Land. Intrigued by its legendary attraction, white settlers repeated the story and Echo Rock continued to be a landmark and caught the attention of steamboat riders, who wanted to visit the spot and hear the echo of their voices. Mr. Merrill and his wife had gone to look for the rock that had been inscribed with its name, ECHO ROCK, and signatures of visitors in the 1870's, according to a picture owned by Dr. G.L. Howe of Brighton. The Merrills left the scene, because they were disappointed that they had found no trace of the old landmark. Soon, they learned from Frank Conner of Hemlock that raising the level of the lake by the City of Rochester had caused shoreline erosion and made the rock slip below the surface of the lake, making the rock's exact location difficult to find.

From the seventy summer residences described in *Up and down the Hemlock* by D. Byron Waite, I chose to write about a few that are uniquely interesting for the general reader and of special interest in relation to the unfolding of this narrative. A complete copy of his book may be obtained by searching Google under Hemlock History. Take a trip back in time. Read the history of the Hemlock Lake area from a writing published in 1883.

If the saying that change is inevitable is true, it applied to Hemlock Lake. because, as early as 1852, it was chosen by the City of Rochester as a reliable source of water supply. By 1876, the first conduit was in operation, but eventually became inadequate and a second conduit was approved in 1891, when development of the shoreline was near its peak. The completion of the railroad in 1895 had stimulated travel to the lake. Contamination became a concern, which culminated in the city's resolve to take over the lakeshore property. The intent was hindered by many complications too numerous to mention here, but gradually lakeshore properties were acquired by the city and the buildings were auctioned off. "Lumber from the buildings, or in some cases, entire buildings can still be found in transported locations in the country side."[79]

By 1947, Rochester had purchased most of the shoreline property and removed the buildings so that it could protect the water supply for its growing population. Fortunately, our family was privileged to enjoy Hemlock Lake as a favorite recreation attraction in the interim period between horse and buggy days and the purchase of all privately owned land by the City of Rochester. Gone were the beckoning hotels and the cottages owned by clergymen, professors, doctors, lawyers, and a cross section of owners from other walks of life. There was a temporary revival of enjoyment of the beautiful natural environment for comparatively few people, who had the privilege of owning a cottage in the last phase of private ownership.

In the early 1920s, my father was one of a group of eight men who bought eight acres of lakefront property on the east side, about two miles from the foot of the lake. The East Lake Road used by horse drawn vehicles had been abandoned for years for lack of maintenance, especially the plank bridges that spanned gullies, in some places quite deep and wide. The condition of the road made the one cottage on the acreage inaccessible by automobile. The alternative was to go by boat from across the lake. My earliest memory of going to the cottage was on a summer day in the year 1925. By way of the West Lake Road, our family had reached a spot on the shore, where we could board a small rowboat propelled by an outboard motor. The boat load of our Father, Mother carrying Doris in her arms, Grandma Gillette, my brother and I, plus provisions for lunch, started in a southeastern direction toward the cottage on the other side of the lake. Miraculously, through rough waters in the center of the lake, my father skillfully navigated and we reached the shore in front of the cottage. I am sure the adults were thankful we had made it safely, while my brother and I were not fully aware of the reason for concern in a small overloaded rowboat that started out smoothly and bounced through waves in the middle of the trip. This was a typical example of possible change of boating conditions from shore to shore, not uncommon on Hemlock Lake. The rest of the day gave us an introduction to our primitive cottage, which was the scene of many happy times in the years to come. Actually, aside from the boat ride and my baby sister's crying, other events have faded beyond recollection, especially the return boat ride in late afternoon, no doubt through calmer waters.

Somewhat later, reaching the cottage by automobile was possible with the restoration of the East Lake Road as far as the southern boundary of property purchased by the eight men. On a day in the middle of the 1920s, my Mother decided to take the family for a ride in our eight passenger touring car. She had recently learned to drive and thought a trip to Hemlock Lake would be a treat for her passengers, including Aunt Jennie, Grandma Gillette, Schuyler and I and our baby sister and possibly Warren Coe, Mother's cousin from Michigan. He had taught her to drive and may have been with us. After a brief stay at the cottage, Mother began the trip home by way of the newly restored East Lake Road which was passable, but required some skillful maneuvering through muddy places, not adequately drained, where quite deep ruts were a challenge for an experienced driver. At one of the trouble spots, the car became mired in the mud and we were stuck. As the nearest telephone was at least a quarter of a mile away, someone walked to call for help, while the rest of us waited to be rescued. In the meantime, when my brother needed a toilet, he relieved himself in the lakeside woods, which exposed him to a dose of poison ivy. In due time, in the darkness of early evening, a man came with a team of horses that pulled the old Cole touring car out of the mud hole and we arrived home with no further delays.

After these first two memorable visits to Hemlock Lake, there were many summers, when a two week stay in the cottage was the high light of the season. Lacking the conveniences we enjoyed at home, electricity and inside plumbing, our summer home was equipped with a Coleman lantern and cook stove, several kerosene lamps, and a two-seated outhouse in the pines at the end of the winding trail on the hillside behind the cottage. To reach the cottage from the East Lake Road, we walked a path on a slight incline, which led to the front porch that extended the width of the building. Directly opposite the centered door was a stairway, giving access to two bedrooms on the second floor. The bedroom on the right provided space for a double bed and a chest of drawers and an extra army cot, if needed, while the room on the left was furnished with army cots, two or more, depending on the number staying overnight. On the first floor, to the right of the stairway, a wood burning stove occupied the center space. There was room for an army cot on either side of the stove and another place on the west side toward the porch. As I remember, my brother and I slept there and Doris also, when she was older. On warm summer nights, we especially loved to sleep on the porch. The mobility of the army cots made changing of sleeping arrangements fairly easy, and if we had favorable weather, we left our cots on the porch during the days and continued to sleep there each night. There were no screens, but mosquitoes never seemed to be a problem.

It might rain, but I do not remember a time when getting wet was a problem. On the other hand, a downpour made the clay road in front of the cottage as slippery as ice. One early morning some fishermen were walking on the road after a time on the lake. While Schuyler, Doris and I were still in bed, we heard the men say "It's just like grease."

Mother served many delicious meals in the dining room located left of the stairs. Her kitchen was in a one story wing attached to the back of the building directly behind the dining room. She cooked on a three burner gasoline Coleman stove. Filling the tank and using a hand pump to supply pressure required some know how, but Mother produced tasty meals that satisfied healthy appetites. The dishes and pots and pans were stored in a small kitchen cupboard. An icebox had space for a limited amount of food. My parents purchased a block of ice in Hemlock and transported it to the cottage when the supply needed to be replenished. A small table top held the washing and rinsing pans for doing dishes with water brought from the lake in pails and heated in a teakettle on the cook stove. We carried our drinking water from home, because we never drank lake water. Our cottage provided the basic needs for shelter and living in an unpretentious manner, but we were happy, while we were there and sorry, when the time came to go home to Lima.

Aside from mealtime and bedtime in the cottage, life at Hemlock Lake was enriched by outdoor activities geared to enjoying the natural environment and by companionship with the Ollerenshaw family, who were our neighbors in their cottage a few hundred feet from ours toward the south. To reach their place we walked south on the road, crossed a bridge that spanned a ravine and arrived at their cabin, which overlooked a point with a beach suitable for swimming. There is where our family went in the water and where all three of us kids learned to swim. How well I remember the thrill of being able to discard the water wings and take off on my own. The Ollerenshaws stayed at the lake all summer. Bill and Laura's children was Irma, Vera, Lila and Harold. Our two families often swam at the same time. My brother and I were glad, when they asked us to join them on hikes down the abandoned road, which we followed as far as we could go, making side trips to explore beaches, especially where the Half Way House used to be. During our first years at the lake, the East Lake Road had not been maintained beyond Ollerenshaw's cottage. Some years later the road was restored a few miles farther. There were days when the Ollerenshaw girls and Harold did not ask us to go with them, because they planned a full day of exploring and climbing gullies and figured the venture would be too strenuous for us. It is wonderful to remember our two families sitting around a beach fire and singing, accompanied by Bill Ollerenshaw playing his guitar. Their family was talented musically. They knew the songs and we learned and joined in whenever we could.

Behind Ollerenshaw's cabin was a ravine that Schuyler, Harold and I climbed frequently, almost daily. At the beginning, the glen was quite wide and offered easy walking beside the flowing stream. As we progressed further, the ravine narrowed and climbing involved switching from one side to the other to find suitable footing or to seek a way around a tree that had fallen across the path of the stream. The final challenge was scaling a cascade, where the water fell over an outcropping of layers of shale, with a fall approximately 75 feet. We climbed by finding footing beside the waterfall. One time I disturbed a nest of bees. Some of them chose to land on my head, but Harold quickly swatted them away and I survived without stings. Beyond the cascade, the steep sides of the glen gradually disappeared giving way to fairly level land. The return trip was down what we called the hogback, a ridge between two gullies, the one we had climbed and another narrower one. During our descent down the ridge, we came to places, where low growing huckleberries grew out of a mixture of loose shale and soil. The end of the hogback brought us to the wider glen, near where we had started behind Ollerenshaws' place. By this time, on a warm summer day, we were ready for a cooling swim in the lake.

A favorite hiking trail was the abandoned road that started a few feet south of Ollerenshaws' cottage and continued southward to the point, where the Half Way House was located and beyond. At first, the width of the old road bed was pretty well defined, providing an easy route for walking, with the exception of the gaping holes, where bridges had deteriorated and proceeding required descending to the stream bed below and ascending to the road level on the other side. In some places, depending on the depth of the gully, the going was easy, at other times, going down and up was more of a challenge. While the road was quite near the lake between points, there was no reason to leave it, but when the trail was some distance from the lake, for sure, there was a beach to be explored and admired, reached by blazing a trail through undergrowth. At that point in our lives, no one had told us what had been built between the lake and the road. For example, at one place, a log cabin was on land next to the lake and a hotel was beside it, attracting visitors who arrived either by horse and buggy or a steamboat. In our day, all that remained, where the Half Way House stood, was a spacious expanse of wooded land and a shale covered beach. Nevertheless, the perfect view up and down the lake and the verdant hillside across the lake had not changed since the days when many came to the site and admired the same view.

Proceeding down the road bed, we walked through more vegetation that had managed to grow there, narrowing the path, which might be fringed with poison ivy. Also, deep and wide gullies, no longer spanned by bridges, were frequent, until we finally came to one so deep that we had difficulty descending and climbing the other side. Usually, this was the turning point, where we retraced our steps to return to the cottage. There was one memorable day, when we abruptly started back after spotting a scantily clad man working in a ravine. We thought he might be a hermit and we did not want to risk an encounter with him. After all, we were just kids, and our bravery in the Hemlock wilderness had its limits, especially if the older Ollerenshaw girls were not with us. I have learned recently that the East Lake Road did extend from head to foot in horse and buggy days, but we never reached the head of the lake, which was likely at least a mile from where we stopped hiking.

Walking on the abandoned road and making side trips to the beaches in the summertime was only a part of what made our Hemlock Lake world special. As kids growing up, we did not fully appreciate that we were learning about the natural environment and having fun at the same time. Unforgettable were day trips to the lake in the springtime, when dogwood bloomed in the woods and wild cherry blossoms decorated the road sides. Imagine the thrill of finding enough white trillium to make a nice bouquet to take home to Lima. This would be unlawful today. Tripping down the hogback in the early spring might be interrupted by a rewarding search for a patch of very fragrant trailing arbutus, blooming after a long winter's rest in the moss covered shale, sprinkled with needles from nearby pines, whose scent mingled with that of the miniature pearly pink and white flowers. It was a time before conservationists had secured protection for these little evergreen plants. However, we looked and admired but did not disturb them in their natural habitat. This was a once in a lifetime experience, never duplicated again for me.

Our early introduction to the study of botany was enriched further by learning to identify the white pines and the hemlocks, their maturing specimens towering above the ground and providing shade that encouraged the growth of many woodland plants. From the banks of the glen, the hemlocks gracefully extended their branches toward the damp places, where ferns thrived, especially the maidenhair. It was fun to dip the foliage in the stream and see it turn into glistening silver. We learned to recognize the white pines by their bundles of five needles in each sheaf, a sure guide for identifying the eastern variety of this evergreen species. On the Hemlock Lake hillsides, the white pines grew in all stages of development from saplings to maturing trees that reached for the sun in competition with their deciduous neighbors. The decomposing leaves beneath the oaks, maples and others nourished the growth of the woodland carpet. Rambling through the woods in the spring would surely lead to discovering Jack-in-the-Pulpit. A little later in the season, a find of yellow lady slippers was a memorable event. My father found some, but we were not with him at the time, and we never learned where they were.

Mother loved flowers, and she had a chance to indulge her fondness one day, when our father took us for a boat ride across the lake. On a point on the west side, Mother spotted a showy growth of sweet peas. Much to her delight, Dad beached the boat and she was able to get out and pick a pretty bouquet to take back to the cottage.

The foregoing account is by no means all inclusive of the many varieties of vegetation that made Hemlock Lake hillsides a natural conservatory, but I have written about a few that made an impression on me, in the days when I was privileged to enjoy them. No doubt, many survive today, in a natural undisturbed state, safely protected by all the no trespassing signs.

Nearing the conclusion of writing about Hemlock Lake, I am adding an assortment of recollections that add to my list of precious memories. Allow me to indulge in a dream of a day, when the weather was not favorable for our usual outdoor activities and we were confined to the cottage. From the protection of the front porch, we observed what was happening, especially to the lake, changed by variations in the weather, since early morning.

As the day progressed, a strong south wind produced white capped waves on the water. Developing from an ominous black cloud, a downpour of rain in the middle of the day drenched the land and the lake. After about an hour, the rain stopped, the wind subsided, and gradually the surface of the lake returned to smoothly rounded waves and finally to gentle ripples. As usual after a rain storm, condensation had caused clouds to rise from gullies across the lake. Mother, attempting to take a late afternoon nap in the upstairs bedroom, was lulled to sleep by the lapping of the gentle waves on the beach. When the sun came out, a glossy smooth surface on the lake lured me to the beach in front of the cottage. This was an ideal time to go for a row boat ride, usually no farther than the point and back. In shallow places along the way, I liked to look through the crystal clear water and see the minnows swimming near the bottom.

Refreshed by her late afternoon nap, Mother prepared supper for a hungry family, my dad, my brother and my sister. After the dishes had been washed and put in the cupboard, Dad took us for a boat ride, which lasted until darkness enveloped the lake and finally, moonbeams danced on the gentle ripples. A falling star made a trail in the nighttime sky. Looking toward the foot of the lake, we saw the flood lights surrounding the home of the Superintendent of the Rochester Water Works of Hemlock Lake. He lived in an impressive two-story, 12 room mansion, built in 1914-15 at a cost of $28,000. Soon after we had observed the display of electricity, dad landed the boat and guided by a flashlight we returned to the cottage, where a Coleman lantern and a kerosene lamp provided light for the remainder of the evening, until bedtime. Since the weather was favorable for sleeping on the porch, Schuyler, Doris and I retired to our army cots. Before our eyelids closed, we saw the moonlight making a glowing path on the surface of the lake and we heard an occasional hoot of an owl, reminding us it was time to drift off to dreamland, while breathing the nighttime air, refreshed by the afternoon rain storm.

Recalling happy days reminds me that our parents let us invite someone for a short stay with us at the lake, either for a day or possibly longer. This gave us opportunities to share good times with our cousins or friends, who walked our favorite trails and swam in the lake with us. We wanted our guests to try one of our favorite pastimes, sliding on boards down a slope covered with fallen pine needles, made slippery by weathering. On the hillside between our cottage and Ollerenshaw's was a dense stand of maturing white pines, making an ideal spot for sliding downhill in the summertime. Leave it to kids to devise ways to have fun.

During my high school years there were two summers, when I invited some of my friends for a week's stay in the cottage. The first time, Dorothy Yorks generously consented to chaperon five girls, including myself. They were Martha Bartlett, Edith Brisbane, Cornie Burton and Marion Dolliver. The second year, Pauline Henessy, our language teacher, consented to stay with us, including two more girls, Margaret Hooker and Willomay McGeary. Our parents sent some food to satisfy our appetites and we took turns preparing meals. Since we did not have the advantage of a car, several times during the week, at least two volunteered to walk to Hemlock to buy groceries. Hiking, swimming and playing games kept us busy. I remember we had fun with an ouija board, which mysteriously answered questions. Perhaps, the most mischievous thing we did was nighttime skinny dipping in the lake in front of the cottage. The Ollerenshaws heard our voices and laughter and guessed what we were doing. As I think about our house parties, I marvel that our parents allowed us to be together for a week with no telephone to call for help in case of an emergency. Fortunately, we survived safely. Basically, our Hemlock Lake world was exclusive and private with no close neighbors except the Ollerenshaws.

Since I do not intend to write more about our stays at Hemlock Lake beyond my high school years, it is with some regret that I must close writing about this chapter in my life. There is more to tell about being there before my father sold the property to the City of Rochester during World War II, but any further additions can not be included within the time limits of this narrative.

More About My Grandparents

In the year 1915, George and Jennie Bartholomew decided to purchase a retirement home on Genesee Street in the village of Lima. Several circumstances must have contributed to their desire to pile their household possessions one more time on a horse drawn wagon and move to Lima, where they had lived on two different farms about nine years before going to another farm outside of Geneseo. Their oldest daughter, Mabel, had married Erson Gillette in 1912 and was living in Lima. Their younger daughter, Jennie, had completed her Geneseo Normal School training and was teaching in Shortsville. Walter, the youngest of the family, had married Marie Welch and was not living at home. At the ages of 65 and 57 respectively, George and Jennie had an empty nest and this was an ideal time for them to leave the demanding and confining work of farm management and enjoy a home in the village, where they might be near their daughter and have a more relaxing life style.

The Bartholomews purchase included 120 rods of land, more or less, dated by deed, August 21, 1915, conveyed by Emogene J. Emmons to George Bartholomew and his wife Jennie. At the time, Genesee Street was sometimes referred to as Railroad Avenue. Mabel Jenks *Outline of the History of Lima* written in 1964, gives a detailed account of historic rail travel, started January 18, 1893 between Lima and Honeoye Falls. The station was on Genesee Street, where the Niagara Mohawk Power

Company substation is now located. The Lima-Honeoye Falls Railroad ran toward the west, across Genesee and Livingston Streets and Harrison Avenue and through the ravine crossing College Street, then a short distance west of Rochester Street through the fields to Honeoye Falls. The equipment consisted of a passenger car and two locomotives. The "Little Road" did enough business to support its maintenance until it had to compete with the Lehigh Valley extension from Honeoye Falls through Lima to Hemlock. In 1898, travel between Honeoye Falls and Lima resumed over the original rail route with trolley service making the four mile, 20 minute trip for 10 cents one way and 15 cents round trip. The business thrived for 15 years, until it was sold and demolished in 1915, the same year that the Bartholomews bought their home on Genesee Street. Years later, Jennie Bartholomew married Carl Warner, who had operated the trolley, before its demise in 1915.

Because I have to depend on my earliest memories, that date from the time when I was about four years old, I have very limited knowledge of my grandparent's life on Genesee Street, in their home, located opposite the Park Street intersection. Their residence was a comfortable two story village house that remains today, with outward appearance basically unchanged. An outside building adequately provided a stable for their horse and storage for their buggy. A garden produced fresh vegetables, with a surplus for canning. There must have been at least one black walnut tree on their property, because Grandma B. made a mixture of ground black walnuts and raisins, that she gave to me and my brother at very early ages. I do not remember her offering us candy. On the other hand, I am told by Cousin Erwin, that Grandpa B. peddled candy on a route traveled in his horse drawn buggy. Erwin said he would see him coming down East Main Road from the village and would say here comes "Shamoo", Bartholomew being too difficult for a three year old to pronounce. Uncle Alfred's purchase of 5 cent Hershey bars for each of the boys was a treat that lasted for some time, one little bite at a time.

After many years of being a farmer, in his retirement, my grandfather had downsized to owning one cow, which he kept at Uncle Edwin Watkins' place diagonally across the street from our cobblestone house on West Main. After feeding and milking his cow, he would stop at our home to visit, usually resting in a chair just inside the kitchen door. Actually my only memory of him was sitting on his lap and combing his hair. I suspect that my grandparents may have sold surplus milk to their neighbors. I do know that Grandma B. made cottage cheese for customers who lived nearby. In the year 1924, while Grandpa B. was milking his cow, he suffered a stroke that caused his death a few days later. Mother went through this difficult time while she was pregnant with my sister, who was born in the fall of the same year.

Following my grandfather's death, Grandma B. continued to live in the house, but eventually she gave up housekeeping. I am unable to identify the exact timing of her whereabouts to the extent that I can write more about her comings and goings. She stayed with us, usually in the summers, when Grandma Gillette was at the farm. She also spent some time with her son's family in Geneseo. Keeping in touch with her brothers and sisters was maintained mainly through yearly family reunions, attended by folks from Michigan, Hornell, N.Y. and Perry, N.Y. I have fond memories of going to several of these gatherings, which were held at the Ellis' farm in Hornell. Aunt Alice was Grandma B's youngest sister, wife of Uncle Carl Ellis and mother of their three sons, Richard, Robert and Thurlow, whose ages, being close to mine and my brother's, made them good companions, whenever we were at the family reunions..

At my age, as I think about Grandma B., I marvel at her dependable ability to manage efficiently so many moves, while she was raising her family. In order of their occurrence, the first was the Bartholomews' migration from Ossian, N.Y. to the Markham farm in Lima. Next they went to the Vary farm, and after a three year stay there they went back to the Markham farm, then owned by Edwin Dibble. After three years there they moved to a farm near

Geneseo. Their last move was back to Lima in 1915. As far as I know, the only disturbing event during all the times they transported their household belongings on a horse drawn wagon was when a lamp fell off the wagon, as they were going down the Ossian hill. In spite of their many changes in residences, Grandma B. maintained a comfortable home for her growing family.

Through the years, Grandma B. had been an excellent seamstress and a good cook. I have a picture of her in her wedding dress which she made by hand in the days before sewing machines. Her delicious pies were always a treat. I have no idea how she made marshmallows, one of her specialties at Thanksgiving time. As a tribute to her, I would say that the same admirable qualities that endeared her as a sister, wife and mother reflected in her attitude toward her grandchildren. She was kind, loving and very much family oriented. I am thankful for the blessing of knowing her.

Writing about Grandma Minnie Gillette involves recording not only my childhood memories, but also a maturing appreciation of her roles as mother, mother-in-law and adoring grandparent. Recall that she became a widow after enjoying only twenty-three years of married life. For sixteen of those years, she had lived in the West Main cobblestone and had shared with my grandfather Schuyler the pride and joy of making additions and improvements within and without that fulfilled their expectations for providing a respectable, comfortable home for the family. After the sudden death of her husband, her attention shifted to being the head of the household for her married son, Erson, and his wife, Mabel, who came to live with her. In the following year, on February 28, 1917, my baby brother joined the family. As far as I know, he had the distinction of being the first to be born in the cobblestone. Mother named him after my grandfather, Ernest Schuyler Gillette. In her new role as Grandmother, she was present to assist with the care of the baby and had the added duties of managing the household during my mother's recuperation, a longer period than experienced by new mothers today. In fact, in the following years, whenever a new grandchild came, Grandma was there to lend a helping hand. This was true for me and my sister and for our five cousins born to Aunt Clara and Uncle Alfred on the farm.

Grandma was an ideal baby sitter while our parents were away from home, either to travel or for social engagements. An example is a time barely within my memory, in 1923, when my Father and Mother were touring parts of New York State. Daddy sent a picture postcard of Ausable Chasm. Included in his brief message to his mother was the question, "How are the kiddies?", the reference being to Schuyler and me, six and four years old respectively.

Grandma had her special ways of showing her love for us. As the years unfolded, preparations for Christmas began early with making gifts for me and my siblings and our cousins on the farm. The whir of her foot-propelled sewing machine in her front bedroom in the cobblestone was a familiar sound. Making flannel nightgowns and pajamas was one of her specialties. As early as I can remember, and for years following, Easter morning found us looking for baskets of home made fondant candy patties, decorated with drizzled chocolate faces. Thanks to our grandmother, we heard the story of *Heidi* read aloud to us, chapter by chapter at bedtime, continuing each night until the end of the story, which we liked so much we wished there were a sequel to follow, but there never was one.

When I told my grandmother I would like to earn some money, she was responsible for teaching me how to make pin cushions that I might sell from door to door. To have a variety, I cut circles about three inches in diameter from different fabrics. By hand stitching around the edge of each piece, I was able to gather the piece to cover a smaller circle of cardboard, about two inches in diameter. The next step was to place two covered card boards together with the shirred edges inside. The finishing touch was whipping the two edges together making a place for inserting pins between the two. Each side of the cushion was a different colored fabric, chosen from Grandma's scrap collection. I am not sure how many I sold at ten cents each, probably no more than twenty. The creative experience was more valuable than the money earned.

Grandma's love of flowers showed in the perennial border bed that she cultivated on the crest of the bank on the east side of the house. In addition, another hobby was identifying wild flowers which she collected from woods and roadsides. Her favorite reference book was *An Illustrated Guide to the Flowering Plants of the Middle Atlantic and New England States* by George T. Stevens, M.D., PhD.

I am glad to write that having known three of my grandparents was a part of my life that I remember with fondness and thankfulness for their love and admirable qualities that made a difference in our lives.

More about my Parents

Getting to know my father, Erson, in this narrative begins with his birth date Aug. 6, 1888, the first son of Schuyler Liddiard Gillett and Minnie Markham Gillett. He received his early education in the private school of Mrs. Sarah Goodrich and the Lima public school and graduated from the Genesee Wesleyan Seminary with the class of 1909 in the business course. While he and his brother, Alfred, were students at the Seminary, one of their professors persuaded them to add an "e" to their name making it Gillette, a change indicative of their French ancestry. As has been noted previously in this account, his courtship of Miss Mabel Bartholomew, also a student at the Seminary, culminated in their marriage on April 12, 1912. After his father Schuyler's death, Erson and Mabel made their home and raised their family in the cobblestone, where all three of their children were born. I cannot pin point the exact time when he began to use his mechanical talent to develop an automobile repair business in his garage in the building that had been used by his father for the Gillett Bottling Works on Livingston Street. Customers not only from Lima but also from neighboring towns as far away as Geneseo relied on his skill and that of the mechanics under his supervision as a garage foreman. His successful business amply provided an income to support his family, especially during the prosperous 1920s.

In his free time, with some outside help, he planted and cultivated a vegetable garden that included an asparagus bed and rows of peas, beets, Swiss chard, string beans, sweet corn, carrots, vegetable oysters, and parsnips. In the fall, several different kinds of apple trees on the property yielded fruit to be picked and stored in the root cellar in the basement of the shop building. A wire enclosure provided space for winter storage of celery (from South Lima), potatoes, apples, etc. Special protection was necessary to guard against an unwanted rat that might invade the cellar.

As has been recorded previously, my father was one of eight men who purchased acreage on the east side of Hemlock Lake, some time in the early 1920s. They were Howard Allen, Bill Ollerenshaw, Leon and Gay Osburn, Harwood Martin, Dr. Kober, Erson Gillette and another whose name I cannot recall. In his spare time, my Father enjoyed fishing with some of these friends, not only in the summer but also through the ice in the winter. Snapshots of plentiful catches are proof that the lake was a good source of supply.

In addition to being a successful business man and a good provider for his family, Erson found time to serve for two terms as village Mayor. Dedicated to supporting civic improvements, during his administration, electric street lights were installed throughout the village and a pumper was purchased for the fire department.

One of my special memories is the day he anticipated, with some uneasiness, meeting Governor Franklin Roosevelt at the White Horse Tavern in East Avon and having to escort his limousine to Lima. The Governor of New York State was on route to the Centennial Celebration of Genesee Wesleyan Seminary. When the Lima officials, including Mayor Gillette, saw him emerging from his car, in his typical congenial manner, he put them at ease, when he said "hello boys". Before Roosevelt's address, my father had the honor of introducing the Governor to the gathering of listeners assembled on the campus lawn in front of Seminary Hall, on that day June 12, 1930, when I was eleven years old. I was not one of the 2,000 who were present at this historic occasion, but was fully aware of my Father's involvement in the events and have a lasting impression of his capabilities on that day, when anticipating anxieties were replaced with pleasure and satisfaction.

Anyone who knew Erson Gillette enjoyed his sense of humor. One story that he liked to tell about his adolescent years was the time he and some of his friends were going on an early morning adventure. I do not remember what they were going to do. They expected Harold Dibble to join them, but he was not an early riser. To make sure Harold would be awake, the night before they tied a long string on his big toe, and hung the string out his bedroom window. The next morning a sudden jerk on the string awakened him. "Dib" lived with his family in the big house east of the cobblestone across the valley.

In the late 1920s, our Fourth of July celebrations were made special by a display of fireworks in our own back yard, before it was illegal to do so in New York state. Some of the neighbors were invited to join us on the back porch of the cobblestone, an ideal viewing stand. My father always bought the fireworks and did the necessary preparation for setting off the skyrockets. Roman candles and pinwheels were part of the display, the latter having been fastened to the corner of the barn. My brother and I had amused ourselves, during the day, with cap guns and Schuyler did have a toy cannon. When we were in our early teens, we happened to be at Hemlock Lake on the Fourth of July. The Ollerenshaws were celebrating with us and we were in front of the cottage, a good position for firing the skyrockets over the lake. Irma was holding a Roman candle and after lighting the fuse, it exploded in her hand causing a severe burn. Needless to say, this was the end of our celebration, because Irma had to be rushed to the nearest doctor in the village of Hemlock. This is a good example of the kind of injuries that eventually led to the prohibition of the sale of fireworks in New York state and other localities in our country.

There is one more story that I want to write about my father. He liked limburger cheese sandwiches. Because my mother could not stand the smell of the cheese in the house, Daddy had to resort to making and eating his sandwiches on the horse block, which was located next to the driveway, at the end of the sidewalk that led to the porch and the side entrance of the house. Gone were the days, when ladies in their high button shoes and ankle length skirts used this convenience to alight from horse drawn buggies. How they managed to ascend to the ground level without the help of a railing was remarkable. Perhaps they were assisted by gentlemen who had ridden in the buggies and had offered their arms for support.

It is impossible to write about my father without including my mother, for the two of them were married for fifty-four years, a partnership in which each supported the other in their roles of husband and wife, provider and homemaker and caring parents. I am amazed, when I think of all the things my Mother did for a growing family. Providing tasty nourishing meals was mainly her responsibility with some help from Grandma, who was with us during the winter months and sometimes at the farm in the summer. When my siblings and I were in school, we went home at noontime for dinner, because Daddy needed a substantial midday meal, after a busy morning in the garage to be followed by more demands on his energy in the afternoon. Except when we had company, we ate our meals at a table in the kitchen.

Mother prepared some desserts during the week, but Saturday was baking day, when she made cookies or cake or both to be used for sweet endings for meals, whenever she had not made something else, which might be one of her delicious pies or a custard or bread pudding. Butternut cake was one of her specialties made with nuts in the batter and the final touch was halves decorating the frosting on the top of her three layer creation. The source of supply was a butternut tree located east of the house at the foot of the hill. In the fall, a cool day after school was an ideal time to gather the nuts, that could be found in groups of two or three nestled in clumps of grass. The hard shells were encased in sticky brownish green husks which dried to a dark brown, after the nuts had been spread to dry.

Three black walnut trees on our property yielded more than one bushel of nuts, but gathering was only the beginning of a process which prepared them for storage. Our father placed a wide board on the east end of the stone foundation of the demolished cow barn. Placing a handful of nuts in their green husks on the board made them ready for shucking with a wooden mallet that smashed the husks one nut at a time. The shucked nuts were shoved from the board into a bushel basket positioned below. Our dad taught us kids how to do all of this and he was pleased to have help with a chore which took time and required patience. Each of us did our share of shuckng, but we took turns and worked one at a time on a Saturday or an afternoon after school. The shucked nuts were ready for spreading to dry before they were suitable for use. The drying area was the floor of the small room behind the main part of the barn. You may be wondering how the family used the black walnuts which had been harvested and carefully prepared for storage. I know my father's favorite nut cracking area was on the wide stone ledge of the furnace cellar window. My Mother made delicious black walnut quick bread. It had a distinctive flavor which made it a family favorite.

Mother's oven was above the burners on the gas fired black iron cook stove. At times she used the natural gas from the well on our property, but the pressure did not last for continuous use and she had to switch to the gas from the gas company. A large kitchen cabinet, occupying space on the north kitchen wall stored baking supplies, flour, sugar, etc. The pantry, that extended from the southeast side of the kitchen, had plenty of shelves for pans of baked goods and other utensils. At the south end of the pantry was a large built-in icebox kept cool by weekly delivery of ice to an outside access reached by the back porch.

Canning was a time consuming summer activity, that produced quarts of vegetables and fruits to be stored on tables in what we called the further cellar, the one beneath the front of the house. Corn, string beans and beets came from Daddy's garden. The fruit canning season began with using ox heart cherries, picked from a tree in the back yard, and later harvesting Bartlett pears from a tree that grew on the slope of the hill toward the shop. Mother made delicious sickle pear pickles from fruit that came from another back yard tree. Also, she made jams and jellies which she stored in a screened free standing cupboard in the further cellar.

The size of the cobblestone required a systematic routine of cleaning on a weekly basis. My mother managed this aspect of housekeeping with special attention to vacuuming the rugs and dusting the furniture, usually on Friday. I remember helping with the dusting and more than once my special chore was washing the cellar stairs. My sister and I shared the back bedroom and it was our responsibility to keep that room neat and clean. Spring house cleaning was an annual event, requiring several weeks for completion. The ceilings and walls had to be brushed for dust and cobwebs. The woodwork in all the rooms must be washed with water to which a small amount of kerosene had been added for disinfecting and cleaning purposes. I did help with some of that detail. At the end of spring housecleaning, every room in the house had been given special attention.

Sewing for the family was a necessity, but it was also a form of relaxation and creative activity that Mother enjoyed. She made my dresses and my sister's and some for herself. In his younger years, she made my brother's waists and knickers. Within my memory, are trips to Rochester to shop at Sibleys or McCurdys for material or patterns. While she searched through the pattern books, I might resort to sitting on the floor for what seemed a long, long time. Lunch in Sibley's basement cafeteria was a treat that we enjoyed, especially hot chocolate topped with plenty of whipped cream. I vaguely remember one time going to the city on the train, which we boarded at the Lehigh station, located east of the Lima village. Riding the bus was our regular means of transportation, until Mother learned to drive and had the confidence to make the trip to the city and back.

Mother was a devoted member of the Lima Presbyterian Church. That she considered church attendance an important part of her children's development was reflected in the fact that all three were baptized, registered on the cradle roll, went to Sunday school and eventually sang in the junior choir. I became a member of the church, when I was ten years old. The example of my Mother's faith and beliefs has been a blessing that has grown more precious in my memory with each passing year. When I was in my early childhood, about five or six years old, I wanted to talk with my Mom about dying and being buried in the ground. She relieved my anxiety by saying that according to the Bible there will come a time when the dead will rise from their graves. Many years later, I discovered an Old Testament statement that was the basis for her comforting words. and it still has faith building meaning for me and many others as well. In Isaiah 26:19 we read "Thy dead shall live, their bodies shall rise." Furthermore, in the New Testament, more details about personal resurrection support a maturing faith. For example in Acts 24:14-15 Paul speaks in his own defense when he says, " I do admit this to you: I worship the God of our ancestors by following that Way which they say is false. But I also believe in everything written in the Law of Moses and the books of the prophets. I have the same hope in God that these themselves have, namely, that all people, both the good and the bad, will rise from death."

As a member of the Ladies Aid Society, she faithfully supported church dinners and bake sales. One of her special contributions, in partnership with Mrs. Klitgord, was promoting and managing flower shows in the fellowship hall, for several days during two successive summers. There were displays of blooms with awards for the best examples in the different categories. Mother loved her flower garden which she expanded as she had more time to enjoy her hobby. Her garden reached its greatest expanse, when she cultivated the side hill of the back yard and the space west of the shop. In addition, she had a wild flower garden on the bank east of the house, about opposite the parlor window. There yellow lady slippers, transplanted from Hemlock Lake, were an attraction that visitors might go to see.

I am sure many mothers deserve medals for their care of their families during illness and ours was a good example. She nursed us through bouts of childhood diseases: whooping cough, measles, and chicken pox. The most demanding and lasting session was the nine weeks that a scarlet fever notice posted on the door indicated that we were quarantined. My brother was the first case, confined to his bed upstairs. My father and I were next. The two of us were in beds in the room west of the living room. When Dr. Kober came to make a house call, he had to put on a gown. Fortunately, Mother, Grandma and Doris did not get the disease and all three patients went through the fever, rash and peeling stages and survived after extended bed rest and recuperation without further complications.

Probably, beginning in the late twenties, Mother belonged to a ladies' bridge club. She thoroughly enjoyed the game and association with her friends. As the years went by, they progressed from auction to contract. An annual event was asking their husbands to join them, when one of the members hosted a dinner party and evening of playing the game. My father attended, rather reluctantly, but his liking for the game did not equal that of Mother's. In addition to bridge playing, another activity she enjoyed was being a member of the Quaerie Club, a group that listened to papers written by members on selected subjects, read at the monthly meetings.

Although both of our parents liked being with their peers for social events, there were many times, when our family had good times together. Especially vivid in my memory are the picnics. A good example are the days that Daddy would come from work to find that Mother had prepared a picnic supper. A ride in the country found us searching for swings and a slide in a schoolhouse yard, where we might gather on a blanket spread on the grass to eat our supper and then be free to use the school's play equipment. We might choose other places for our picnics, but schoolhouse yards were our favorites.

The stock market crash in 1929, followed by the Great Depression, made changes in my father's source of income, that had adequately supported our family during the prosperous 1920s Several factors contributed: the failure of the Lima bank, my father's loss of money in investments, plus the decline of the garage business, that reflected the economic problems which became widespread in the country. To supplement his earnings he undertook a new adventure for him. He established a Plymouth and DeSoto sales agency in Lima. His sales room occupied space next to Hayes and Andrews show room on West Main Street. He had some success with the business during the 1930s. To help relieve the effects of the depression on our family income, Mother began to make bread which she sold directly to some Lima residents and she also supplied local grocery stores with her bread. Soon she expanded her business to include other baked goods: coffee cakes, pies, cookies, cupcakes, etc. that occupied shelves in the Lima stores and eventually in Honeoye Falls. Her bakery equipment was in the first cellar in the basement of the cobblestone and included a large multilevel oven, work tables and other conveniences necessary for her business.

The affectionate relationship between my mother and her sister, Jennie, brings to mind many treasured memories of a dearly loved member of the family. Jennie never had children of her own, but as a devoted aunt she made a difference in the lives of her nieces and nephews. She always remembered us at Christmas time with gifts that also included something for our cousins. When she had vacations from her teaching position in Lakewood, Ohio, she was with our family for many good times.

From her parents' farm, she had walked to school at the Geneseo Normal School, where she received two years of training for teaching in the elementary grades. After graduation she had a teaching position in Shortsville and met another teacher,

Emma VanDuser, who became her lifelong friend. I do not know exactly how long they taught in Shortsville, but probably within a year or so, the two friends decided to accept positions in Lakewood, Ohio. They continued to be employed there, until their retirement some forty years later. Aunt Jennie taught sixth grade and I think Emma's grade was fifth. For some years, the two friends kept house together in a rented apartment. In the year 1924, Aunt Jennie bought a Dodge car, which she drove to Lima to be with her family at Christmas time and in the summer to spend her vacation in Lima. During the years there were many changes that affected Emma and Jennie's lives. Emma's aging Mother went to live with her daughter in Lakewood, until Mrs. VanDuser's death. Aunt Jennie married Carl Warner. Their marriage changed their living arrangements. First, they lived in Lima during the summer vacations and later they had a year around home in Cleveland, until Aunt Jennie retired and they purchased a house in Lima. Sometime after Aunt Jennie married Carl, Emma married Mother's cousin Warren Coe. Until their retirement, their home was in Cleveland and they spent the remaining years in Florida.

Part of my mother's close connection with her family was keeping in touch with her brother Walter, who had married Marie Welch and built a home on Livingston Street in Geneseo. Their children, with their birth dates were Edgar George-1917; Spenser Jay-1919; Ida Marie-1922; Walter, Jr.-1925 and Janet Evangeline-1941. Uncle Walter worked in the Retsof salt mine until his retirement. To supplement their income, Aunt Marie did washings and ironings for some of the affluent families in Geneseo. We saw the Bartholomews at family gatherings, reunions and picnics, and during visits in each others homes, togetherness for which I am grateful, especially getting to know our cousins. How well I remember the delicious New Year's Day dinners Aunt Marie served to us, usually roast pork with all the trimmings.

The foregoing account of my parents and our days, when they showed us tender loving care, are by no means all inclusive of the many things they did for us in the years when we were growing up. At this point in our lives, we could honestly say there was no other place like home, that being within the walls of a cobblestone house, the shelter for several generations before our time.

School Days

In the year 1907, Lima's school district no.9 built a two story four room grade school on College Street to replace the building on the site of the present Town Hall. In September 1924, my brother started first grade in Miss Coykendall's class. By this time, the school had been remodeled to accommodate four years of high school and an annex had been added to the back of the building for seventh and eighth grades. Although I was only 4 years 4 four months old, I wanted to go to school with Schuyler. I was so insistent that Mother called the teacher. Fortunately, her wise advice was that I wait another year. Consequently, in September, 1925, my brother took me with him to start my first day, which went well, until almost time to leave, and I cried, because I thought Schuyler was going home without me. In those days, Miss Coykendall taught first, second and third grades, somewhat less demanding than the responsibilities of teaching in one room schools, which still existed in Lima's outlying districts. In those first three years, under our teacher's expert instruction, we learned to read and to write, the latter according to the Palmer Method. We were taught the basics of arithmetic, addition, subtraction. and multiplication. At the end of the first year, dismissal time for vacation depended on being able to recite the alphabet. I was not one of the first to be excused for the summer, but did have that privilege a day or so later.

Miss Coykendall was a strict disciplinarian, who used a rubber tube to deal with unruly behavior. How well I remember her coming down the aisle with that thing in her hand and hoping I was not the one deserving punishment. At any rate, her actions served to remind all of us we better behave or suffer the consequences. At dismissal time, Miss Coykendall expected her classes to leave the school in a straight line following the center crack to the end of the front sidewalk of the school.

After finishing third grade, pupils went to Miss O'Brien's room for fourth, fifth and sixth grades. It did not take long to learn that her method of maintaining order was a crack with a ruler on the knuckles of the one misbehaving. After I had been in her room for most of fourth grade, she suffered a crippling injury from a bad fall and was unable to continue teaching. Her replacement was Mrs. Marjorie Leary who became my favorite teacher.

At the end of the school year, each elementary class was expected to perform at closing exercises in the Lima Town Hall. When our class was being promoted from Mrs. Leary's room, she taught us to dance the minuet as our part in the program. We were dressed in appropriate costumes, the girls in lace-trimmed dresses made by our mothers and the boys in suitable waists and knee high pants and shoes trimmed with large silver buckles, made of cardboard covered with tinfoil. Boy and girl couples followed a routine of steps and bows, accompanied by Miss Belle Chapin playing the piano. She was the music teacher, who came to our rooms to give music instruction on a weekly schedule. After each grade had taken part in the program, students received certificates of promotion from one grade to another, and those who had the highest average in their respective grades were awarded 2 dollar gold pieces.

Mrs. Emily Bacon taught seventh and eighth grades in the annex that extended from the south end of the main building. I have fond memories of her ability to instruct and maintain discipline with a steady and caring skill that made her a good teacher. A relaxing time in her room was when she read aloud, chapter by chapter the book *Anne of Green Gables*. This stimulated a liking for the story which continues to this day. Another lasting memory is our response as eighth graders to the 1932 tragic kidnapping of the Lindberg baby, their first child, Charles Augustus, Jr. Before the mystery of his disappearance had been solved, Mrs. Bacon asked us to write a story about "How I Found the Lindberg Baby."

During my eighth grade year, I was excused extra days for Thanksgiving recess to go to Cleveland to visit Aunt Jennie, who taught sixth grade in the Lakewood elementary school. I was allowed this privilege but had to promise that I would stand before the class, when I returned, and give an account of what I did during my absence from school. Aunt Jennie made sure my visit included a trip to the Cleveland Museum of Natural History and the Cleveland Museum of Art and other experiences that I might describe in my talk, including President James A. Garfield's Memorial. He was assassinated on July 2, 1881.

Four years of high school in the same building, where I had been since first grade, led to getting good grades and earning a regents diploma. The required subjects had been English, algebra, geometry, Latin, French, history, biology and chemistry. Study halls were in the second floor room at the left of the stairs. Also, some subjects were taught there. The library was in the little room at the head of the stairs. The right side of the second floor was divided into two class rooms. The principal's office was in the front room, facing College Street. Science classes were in the basement. Because there was no gymnasium, physical education was not part of the high school course, but those who were interested could go to basketball practice in the town hall and train to be on the team competing in games with other schools. I was never chosen to take part in basketball practice, so my high school courses did not include athletics. The teachers that I can identify with the subjects they taught were Miss Slattery, English; Miss Hennessy language; Miss Schield, mathematics; Mr. Nugent, history and Mr. Edgett, principal, who taught chemistry in our senior year. While we were taking regents in June, 1936, we could hear the workmen beginning construction of the new combination grade and high school to replace the one where we had spent twelve years. In other words, ours was the last senior class that received all of their under graduate education in the old building which was demolished to make way for the new school completed in 1937 and ready for use in that year.

In addition, our graduation exercises in the Lima Town Hall have historical significance, because ours was the last class to receive our diplomas on that stage. The following quote from an article in the "Lima Recorder" gives a description of what happened that night in June,1936. It is worth quoting, since some of the details have faded from my memory and the following eye witness account should be preserved for future reference.

The head lines of the article are as follows: "Nine Seniors Are Given Diplomas, Colorful Exercises Mark Close of L.H.S. School Year". The reporters description of the event continues.

The 18th annual commencement of Lima High School closed Monday evening with the following nine seniors receiving their diplomas from Principal C. C. Edgett: Janet M. Davis, Raymond H. Delles, Margaret M. Gillette, Vernon A. Gillette, William F. McGeary, M. Eileen McSweeney, Nancy B. Osborne, Mildred E. Samborski and H. Onalee White. Class members, faculty and school board were grouped on the town hall rostrum during the ceremonies.

Program opened with a march by Miss C. Belle Chapin, invocation by the Rev. Jas. A. Hamilton; salutatory, "Indian Legends," Nancy Osborne; song, "Annie Laurie," Presbyterian young men's quartet; address "Possessed of a Dream," the Rev. Robert Kazmayer, Rochester; song, "O Dry Those Tears," Cecelia E. Costello; valedictory, "Character, the Cornerstone of Success," Margaret M. Gillette; benediction, the Rev. H. A. Long, Hemlock.

Prof. Edgett, completing his first year as principal, made an address of dramatic earnestness, as he urged the seniors to watch their character building, and exhorted parents to give the school loyal support. He announced a four-number entertainment course to be given next fall for benefit of the school. Miss Gillette's valedictory was a model in text and delivery. She and her cousin Vernon are the only members of the class who started in the school as 1st grade pupils of Miss Coykendall. The Rev. Mr. Kazmayer, youngest Methodist minister in Rochester, proved an ideal guest speaker and doubtless he will be called here again.

Sunday evening's baccalaureate service was one of the best in the school's history, the speaker, the Rev. John M. Ball, St. Rose church pastor, taking less than ten minutes for his theme which ended with the familiar, heart-searching quotation, "To thine own self be true." The talk was well supplemented by the song-prayer "Ave Maria" sung by Miss Mary R. O'Connell, class of 1932, with Miss C. Belle Chapin at the piano. The girl's glee club sang and H. J. Chapman gave the prayer and benediction.

The seniors' class night, Saturday, was featured by the class prophecy given by Onalee White without notes or prompting. Mildred Samborski, class poet, also spoke from memory. V. Gillette, one of the trio of young farmers of the class, wrote an excellent class history, and R. Delles of the Plank road did equally well with the class will. Presentation of class gifts by Eileen McSweeney and Janet Davis kept the crowd in an uproar. The class key was presented by President Wm. McGeary to junior head, John M. Bartlett, who responded with junior frankness.

Principal Edgett announced that the school board had discontinued giving scholastic prizes and athletic letters, and the only cash award of the evening was the $5 American History of Lima D.A.R., which was won by valedictorian Margaret Gillette. Perfect attendance certificates went to Mona McNeilly, 7th grade; Audrey Crouse, 9th grade; Eugene Hogan and Clifford Chatterton 10th grade; Anna Lawrence, 11th grade.

As usual, grade night exercises Friday drew the largest crowd of the week-end, although the air was mid-Julyish.

An operetta in two acts, "What's the Matter with Sally?" was delightfully given by grades 1 to 6. Cast headliners were Lois Kober, Doris Gillette, Bernard Morasco, Mildred Brooks, Mary Peck, Eleanor Sherman, Sally Barber and Leora McNeilly.

Specialty numbers were furnished by Lima's first "Tom Thumb Band," which under the training of Miss Coykendall, primary teacher, made surprising melody. Theresa Harvey, Barbara Adams and Shirly White gave dance numbers. An older pupil Melvin Semell, pleased with cowboy songs, appearing in costume.

This is the end of the article in the June 26 "Lima Recorder" which gave the foregoing account of the events of graduation week including the Friday grade exercises, Saturday Senior class night, Sunday evenings baccalaureate and finally the Monday night graduation.

My preparation for that memorable graduation night had involved choosing a subject for my valedictory speech and writing the lines which were to be memorized word for word. Prof. Edgett gave me some good advice, when he suggested that I might write about our class motto, "Character is the Cornerstone of Success" This seemed like a good idea and I chose to speak about Jane Addams whose life was an ideal example of how her character had contributed to her success. She was the founder of Hull House, in Chicago, one of the first social settlement houses in the United States. A book from the Lima Public library was a helpful guide, giving me facts about her life that indicated her character had a strong influence on her success in reaching her goals dedicated to helping others. I am sorry I do not have a copy of my speech and have to depend on my memory to quote some of the beginning and the end. The introduction explained that several months before our class had chosen their motto. Then I said, "Let us consider the life of one person, whose character alone shaped the fulfillment of her one ideal, an earnest desire to promote fellowship among men." I chose to mention something about her youth, followed by some of her accomplishments in her adult life, as a famous social worker. The exact wording of the text has faded from my memory. As part of my concluding thoughts about our lives beyond our high school years, I remember saying, "There will be forced landings, times when uncontrollable powers will have full sway. Forced landings are never for long, and the renewed ascents are likely to be twice glorious." Would my classmates agree that my youthful idealistic optimism has stood the test of time, perhaps with the exception of the phrase, "forced landings are never for long". Here I am again, searching for concluding words to finish this narrative, seventy years after that memorable night in June 1936. Yes, the intervening years brought failures replaced by successes and threatening depths of despair replaced by soaring to new heights. My knowledge of John Barnard's life and the lives of my ancestors leads me to believe that they were able to express similar thoughts in their aging years. As I come to the end of this story, my desire is to finish with a prayer taken from the poem that inspired the title and introduction. With the hope that all of us will eventually make that final glorious ascent to our heavenly home, I quote the appropriate words written by May Brahe in 1927: "Bless us all that we may be Fit, O Lord, to dwell with Thee, Bless us all that one day we May dwell, O Lord with Thee."

Lima School

Bibliographpy

[1] Rundel Library. 10/30/02<http://www.monash.edu.au/NFRAM/nfmabrah.htm

[2] Bertha Kropp Cable, *A Cloud of Witnesses* (Rome, New York, 1993), p. 24.

[3] Cable, p. 32

[4] Cable, p. 41

[5] Cable, p. 43

[6] Cable, p. 61

[7] Cable, p. 61.

[8] Cable, p. 61

[9] Lockwood R. Doty, *History of Livingston County* (Jackson, Michigan, 1902), p. *722*

[10] Doty, p. 722

[11] Frances S. Gotcsik, *Two Hundred Years of Presbyterian Life in the Lima Community* (Lima 1995), p. *1*.

[12] Wm. R. McNair, *Presbyterian Church, Lima, Livingston Co., New York 1795-1895 Historical Sketch* (Philadelphia, 1895), p.*6*.

[13] McNair, p. 6.

[14] McNair, p. 6.

[15] McNair, p. 6.

[16] McNair, p. 6 & 7.

[17] McNair, p. 7.

[18] McNair, p. 7.

[19] McNair, p. 6.

[20] McNair, p.7.

[21] McNair, p. 10.

[22] Cable, p. 48.

[23] Mabel Furner Jenks, *Outline of the History of Lima* (Lima, New York, 1964), p. *17*.

[24] Lefferts A. Loetscher, *A Brief History of the Presbyterians* (Philedelphia, Penn., *1938*), p. *16*.

[25] Gotcsik, p. 2.

[26] Cable, p. 76.

[27] Cable, p. 76.

[28] Carl S. Schmidt, *Cobblestone Masonry* (Scottsville, New York 1966), p. 34.

[29] McNair, p. 12.
[30] McNair, p. 13.
[31] Doty, p. 102.
[32] McNair, p. 13.
[33] Loetscher, p. 18.
[34] Bertha Bortle Beal Aldridge, *Gillette Families* (Victor, New York, 1955), p.11.
[35] Loetscher, p. 29.
[36] Loetscher, p. 29.
[37] Loetscher, p. 29.
[38] Loetscher, p. 29.
[39] Aldridge, p. 15.
[40] Aldridge, p. 15.
[41] John Warner Barber, *Connecticut Historical Collections* (Hanover, N.H., 1999), p..124.
[42] Barber, p. 124.
[43] Barber, p. 125-126.
[44] Aldridge, p. 15.
[45] Barber, p.127.
[46] Aldridge, p. 15.
[47] Barber, p. 127.
[48] Barber, p. 102.
[49] Barber, p. 102.
[50] James H. Smith and Hume H. Cole, *History of Livingston County* (Syracuse, N.Y, 1881), p. 477.
[51] Smith and Cole, p. 478.
[52] The World Book Encyclopedia (Chicago 1962) Vol. 3, p 492
[53] The World Book Encyclopedia, Vol. 11, p. 286.
[54] Rev. Joseph R. Page, "The Model Gospel Minister"
[55] Page.
[56] Page.
[57] Page.
[58] Page.
[59] Frances Gotcsik, " Barnard Cobblestone House," Building Structure Inventory Form, 1988, p. 5.
[60] The World Book Encyclopedia (Chicago, 1962) Vol.7 p.53
[61] Unknown

[62] Nellie Talbot and E.O.Excell, "I'll be a Sunbeam," (Hope Publishing Co.).

[63] Leland LeBrun, "Diamonds in the Rough", (Livonia Gazette, 1987).

[64] LeBrun.

[65] LeBrun.

[66] LeBrun.

[67] LeBrun.

[68] D. Byron Waite, *Up and Down the Hemlock, 1883*

[69] Waite.

[70] Arch Merrill, "Diving Suites Sound Like a Good Idea on Echo Rock Visit" (Democrat and Chronicle, 1953).

[71] Waite.

[72] Waite.

[73] Waite.

[74] Waite.

[75] Waite.

[76] Waite.

[77] Waite.

[78] Waite.

[79] LeBrun.